IMAGES
of America

DETROIT'S HISTORIC FORT WAYNE

In 1892, Col. Simon Snyder of the 19th Infantry Regiment was Fort Wayne's commanding officer. Promotions were slow in the old army. John W. Phelps graduated from West Point in 1836, and wrote to his sister about his assignment to the U.S. 4th Artillery, saying "it is called the immortal Regiment—there are lieuts in it with grey heads, fine prospects for me!" (Detroit Historical Museum.)

On the cover: The main gate to Fort Wayne changed in location and design many times during the fort's active service as a military post. This 1905 gate was moved when it was unable to accommodate the size of mechanized military convoys. The sandstone carvings of a mortar and cannon atop the pillars were moved to the scarp of the fort and now decorate the vehicular entrance to the star fort that was added in 1938. (Detroit Historical Museum.)

IMAGES
of America

DETROIT'S HISTORIC
FORT WAYNE

James Conway and David F. Jamroz

ARCADIA
PUBLISHING

Published by Arcadia Publishing
Charleston, South Carolina

Printed in the United States of America

Library of Congress Catalog Card Number: 2006939093

For all general information contact Arcadia Publishing at:
Telephone 843-853-2070
Fax 843-853-0044
E-mail sales@arcadiapublishing.com
For customer service and orders:
Toll-Free 1-888-313-2665

Visit us on the Internet at www.arcadiapublishing.com

To Carolyn, Gayle, and Karen.

CONTENTS

ACKNOWLEDGMENTS

Since historic Fort Wayne was constructed in 1841, thousands of soldiers, Detroit public servants, and volunteers contributed tens of thousands of hours to preserve its history and facilities. Without their hard work and love of the old fort, this book would not have been possible. The Historic Fort Wayne Coalition, National Society Colonial Dames of America in Michigan, Friends of Fort Wayne, the Fort Wayne Guard, and many local public and commercial enterprises have dedicated time and resources preserving the history found in this book. The Detroit Historical Museum's Collections Research Center, and the Detroit Public Library's Burton Historical Collection offer a wealth of information on the fort. The majority of the images in this book were provided by them. Other images came from the collections of Wayne State University's Walter P. Reuther Library, the U. S. National Archives and Records Administration (NARA), the Library of Congress American Memory Collection, the Michigan State Archives, Travel Michigan, and the family collection of a Fort Wayne supporter donated in memory of all the veterans who have passed through the fort.

We thank our editor Anna Wilson of Arcadia Publishing for providing her professional expertise, and most importantly, her enthusiastic support. Author and collections curator Marianne Weldon provided access to the archives of the Detroit Historical Museum, and Detroit Historical Society executive director Robert Bury was generous in granting us permission to reproduce those images. B and B Studios provided photographic support for the oversize images used.

There are many who, through their commitment to the fort's history, established the pathways to this book. Prominent among them are retired fort curator Dr. William Phenix, Thomas Berlucchi, Will Eichler, Bode Morin, Matt Merta, Linda and Robert Zaber, Genevieve Jamroz, Ed Badstuber, John Bluth, Michele Cierniak, Robbie Clifton, Michael W. R. Davis, Edwin Duda, Ted Dutkiewicz, Bill Hagen, Kevin Heise, Michael Kendra, Tony Krauss, Richard Lebeck, Joseph Lizor, Don Longo, Jim Mackenzie, Patience Nauta, Lt. Gen. Dave Palmer, Mark Patrick, John Polacsek, Doug Rogers, Geoff Rose, Chris Schuler, Leo Schuster, Albert St. Louis, David Schneider, Tom Stone, Tyler Strickler, Steve Titunik, Deborah Thunberg, Mary J. Wallace, Dr. William Vecchioni, Ridge Vincent, David Ward, Michael Webster, and Dr. Dennis Zembala. All provided the literary example, encouragement, and enthusiasm that made this book possible. We wish the City of Detroit Recreation Department under director Loren Jackson, deputy Lawrence Hemingway, manager Edith Worthy, and their staff every success in their continuing operation of the fort. Finally, to our wives, and Karen and Matt, we give thanks for their patience and continuing support.

INTRODUCTION

Located on a strategic bend of the Detroit River, Historic Fort Wayne has guarded the international strait separating Detroit from Windsor, Ontario, Canada, since the 1840s. It is Detroit's third and last fort built to control the use of the key connecting waterway in the Great Lakes system. The fort is located on 96 acres. Since the 1970s, 83 acres, the star fort, and many buildings have been operated as a museum and recreation site by the City of Detroit. The remaining acres comprise the Army Corps of Engineers boatyard.

The origins of Fort Wayne begin with a conflict on the Michigan-Ontario border in the late 1830s known as the Patriot War. Local residents of the period remembered the War of 1812 a few decades earlier when Detroit had been captured by the British Army and held for over a year. Indeed, it is the only major American city to have this distinction. Canadian and American rebels organized in the late 1830s to free Canada from British rule. Battles were fought in 1838 along the Detroit River. American troops were mustered to suppress the American volunteers and enforce the nation's stated neutrality in that conflict. Concurrently the United States government realized Detroit had no counterpart to British Fort Malden down the Detroit River at Amherstburg, Ontario, to resist a British attack on American soil.

A major effort began to fortify strategic locations along the northern border. In 1841, Congress appropriated the funds to build a chain of 14 forts including a fort at Detroit. Soon afterwards, the army sent Lt. Montgomery Meigs to buy the strategic riverfront farm location three miles below Detroit in Springwells Township and plan a square bastioned defensive fortification. Construction began in 1843 and was completed in 1851 at a cost of $150,000. The army named the new post in honor of Gen. "Mad" Anthony Wayne, a hero of the American Revolution, whose troops had taken American possession of Detroit from the British in 1796. Peaceful relations were restored with British Canada and Fort Wayne stood unused with only a watchman on guard for its first decade of existence.

After the attack on Fort Sumter in Charleston, South Carolina, in 1861, Pres. Abraham Lincoln asked for 75,000 troops from the northern Union States. Two weeks later, the Michigan 1st Volunteer Infantry Regiment was mustered into Federal service at Fort Wayne. During the rest of the Civil War, the fort served as a mustering center for more Michigan units destined for battles with the Confederacy. Michigan veterans returned to Fort Wayne to recover from wounds and illnesses. Fears of Confederate raids coming from Canada, whose parent country sympathized with the South, gave the fort a new strategic importance. More federal funds were allocated to rebuild the crumbling wooden walls of Fort Wayne with brick and concrete, seven and a half feet thick, in the 1860s.

With the end of the Civil War, the fort assumed the role of a garrison post. Infantry regiments rotated from the western frontier for rest and recruitment. Companies, supplied from Detroit's fort, also staffed the outlying Michigan posts at Port Huron (Fort Gratiot), Mackinac Island (Fort Mackinac), and Sault Ste. Marie (Fort Brady). Army units from the fort went overseas to fight in the Spanish American War in Cuba and the Philippines.

With the rise of the American automobile industry, Detroit assumed a new importance in the replacement of horses and mules with motor vehicles for America's military transportation needs. Although still used by infantry units as a garrison post until 1920, Fort Wayne began its new function as a base for army motor supply. Beginning in World War I, the fort's role in the acquisition of cars, trucks, and spare parts for America's military grew, reaching its zenith during World War II. During World War II, Fort Wayne's facilities were greatly expanded. Major office and shipping buildings were built on the riverfront. Seven warehouses were constructed to house the thousands of tons of vehicle parts that moved through the facility on a daily basis. An army of 2,000 mostly civilian workers provided the woman and man power to supply the equipment to make victory possible. Other workers, controlled from Fort Wayne, operated the vehicle storage and shipping facility at the Michigan State Fairgrounds and the Port of Detroit docks and waterfront warehouses. Detroit became known as the arsenal of democracy, recognition that the city and Fort Wayne made key manufacturing and supply contributions to winning the Second World War.

With the beginning of the Cold War era, the fort gradually lost its motor supply function. It served as the supply base for the anti-aircraft batteries protecting metro-Detroit during the 1950s. When the guns were replaced by Nike missiles in the 1960s, Fort Wayne became the launch control and supply base for the missile batteries. Rumors have it that some of the missiles had nuclear warheads. The fort continued to serve as the armed forces entrance station for Michigan. It was a role the Springwells site had performed since militia camped there while being organized for the Black Hawk War by the garrison at the Detroit barracks. Thousands of enlistees and draftees were given military physicals and swore their oaths of allegiance upon entering service during the Korean War and Vietnam War eras.

The original bastioned fort continued to serve as a storage facility until the end of World War II. It had been recognized as a site of historic and architectural significance in the 1930s by the Depression-era program, the Historic American Building Survey. During the Great Depression architects and historians were employed to record its design resulting in 14 pages of drawings on its buildings and fortifications. In 1949, the star fort and barracks were turned over to the City of Detroit's Historical Commission to be operated as a military museum. In 1971, the Interior Department offered the remaining property to the City of Detroit to expand the museum with additional 19th and early 20th century buildings. The Detroit Historical Museum gradually opened a number of restored buildings to the public and installed a major collections center in one of the large warehouses.

After 1991, funding for the fort declined along with the City of Detroit's and the Detroit Historical Museum's budgets, and the fort closed until 2001. It has reopened on summer weekends and for special events only. A master plan for development and future use of the fort was completed in 2005. The following year, fort operations were turned over to the City of Detroit Recreation Department which continues to keep it open for public and special event use. The Detroit Historical Society, now operating the Detroit Historical Museum, keeps the bulk of its city-owned museum collections in a secure storage facility at the fort. Two private organizations, the Friends of Fort Wayne and the Historic Fort Wayne Coalition, provide monetary and hands-on support to assist in the maintenance and restoration of the property.

One

DETROIT CITY ON THE STRAITS

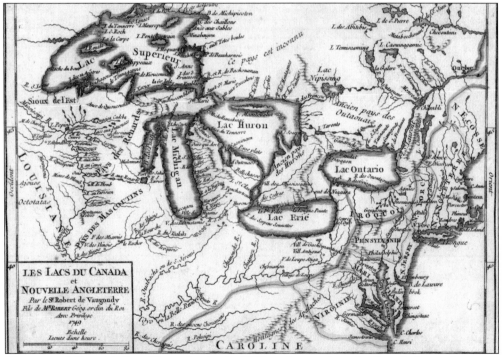

The story of Detroit's Fort Wayne begins in 1700 to the north at the French fur trading post, Fort de Buade, near St. Ignace, Michigan. The French commander viewed the growing British presence in the region with concern. He wanted to establish a French presence further south to counter the advancing British and their Iroquois allies. Protecting the territory of New France and its lucrative fur trade was at stake. (Detroit Historical Museum.)

Capt. Antoine De La Mothe Cadillac was controversial. He commanded the French garrison and ran a fur trading business. The use of liquor in negotiations with Native Americans led to difficulties with the Jesuit priests who saw it as interfering with their efforts to convert the tribes. Overcoming their powerful influence in the French government, Cadillac gained approval to build a fort at the straits connecting Lakes Erie and Huron. (Burton Collection.)

Cadillac's engineers selected a high point of land along a narrow point in the river for the fort and construction began in July 1701. The fort was named for Jerome Phelypeaux, Compte de Pontchartrain, minister for colonial affairs. The settlement growing up at the fort was known as the Village at the Straits (ville de troit). As French families moved into the area the permanent settlement was simply called Detroit. (Detroit Historical Museum.)

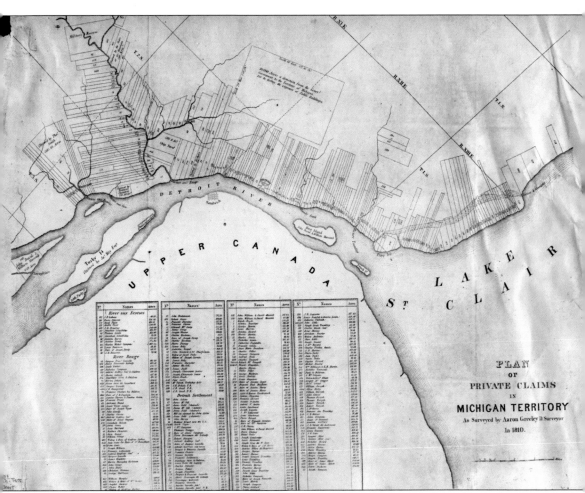

Early Detroit was a fur trading and farming community. The protection of the fort and river transportation was critical to the settlers. As a result, each farmer was given a narrow strip of land on the river that extended back two or three miles. Known as ribbon farms, these belts of land afforded the farmers security from Fort Pontchartrain and the ability to transport furs and produce to market. (Detroit Historical Museum.)

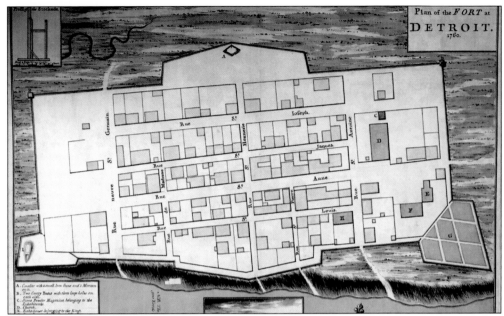

French governor Pierre Francois de Rigaud, Marquis de Vaudreuil-Cavagnal, surrendered the colony of New France to British forces in September 1760. Included in the surrender was the fort at Detroit. As French troops departed, British soldiers took possession of the town. The village had grown to a population of 2,000 with 300 buildings. England would occupy Detroit after the final borders of the United States were established following American independence in 1783. (Detroit Historical Museum.)

United States forces under the command of Capt. Moses Porter arrived in July 1796 to accept the transfer of Detroit from a British army caretaker detachment. After signing over government property to the Americans, the British commander removed his troops to Fort Malden near Amherstburg, Ontario. Americans and British now faced each other across a new international border. Detroit was an American settlement, but the population remained largely French speaking. (Detroit Historical Museum.)

The 32-mile-long Detroit River developed into an important transportation route for commercial traffic with the introduction of steam ships. With completion of the Erie Canal, Detroit became an international port. By the 1850s, shipping was the city's largest industry. Shipments of agricultural products, wood, coal, ore, stone/aggregates, and general cargoes helped establish the city as a transportation center leading the way to Detroit becoming a manufacturing center. (Detroit Historical Museum.)

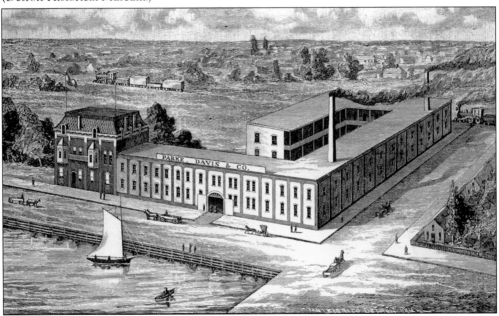

Detroit's economy grew in phases. It was established as a fur trading center but soon assumed a commercial role as an export point for Michigan's agricultural and natural resources. With the Civil War, the city transitioned to a manufacturing center for such items as ships, rail cars, and pharmaceuticals. It would remain a globally-recognized leader in the manufacture of durable goods throughout most of the 20th century. (Silas Farmer's *History of Detroit*.)

In 1898, Ransom Olds began manufacturing automobiles in Detroit. From this beginning, the mass manufacture of cars, trucks, vans, and sport utility vehicles for commercial, private, and military applications led to Detroit's becoming the automobile capital of the world. Its manufacturing base produced such prodigious volumes of vehicles and other war material during World War II that it earned recognition as the arsenal of democracy. (Detroit Historical Museum.)

More than 300 years after Cadillac's Fort Pontchartrain formed the Detroit skyline, a 73-story, 1,400 room hotel sided by four 39-story office buildings was evidence of the city's renaissance. Over the centuries, three military forts—Fort Pontchartrain, Fort Shelby, and Fort Wayne—were integral elements of the city's defense and played their roles in its economic development. The forts reflect Detroit's long cultural and economic history. (Detroit Historical Museum.)

14

Two

DEFENDING THE STRAITS

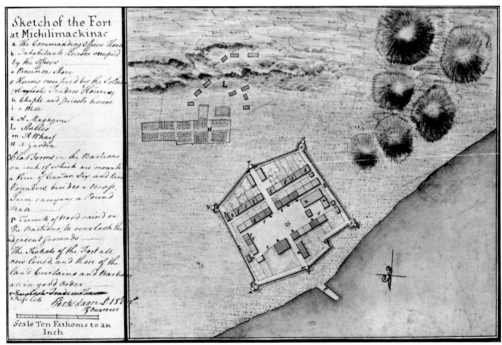

The French first established a military presence in the region at the Straits of Mackinac, a strategic body of water connecting lakes Michigan and Huron. Fort de Buade was constructed in 1683 at the unfortified site of a Jesuit mission established by Fr. Jacques Marquette near the present-day city of St. Ignace. Fort de Buade probably served more as a supply center for fur traders than a military post. Fort Michilimackinac put a French military presence at the straits in 1715. French troops departed in 1761 after the British gained control of the area. During Pontiac's Uprising in 1763, most of the garrison was killed when native forces took control of the fort. Chief Pontiac's forces occupied the fort for nearly a year. The British later abandoned Fort Michilimackinac when they moved to nearby Mackinac Island in 1781. (Detroit Historical Museum.)

British entry into the region caused the commander at Fort de Baude, Antoine de la Mothe Cadillac, to request permission from King Louis XIV, Le Roi Soleil, to move further south to counter that threat to French fur trading with the Native Americans. In 1701, Cadillac moved a French garrison to the straits connecting lakes Huron and Erie. The new fort would be constructed for military control of this strategic waterway. Cadillac described the fort to Count de Pontchartrain, Minister of Marine, for whom it was named: "Our fort is of one mile square, without the bastions, located very advantageously upon an elevation separated from the river by an easy incline of about 40 feet which forms a glacis, very agreeable. They took care to put it on the narrowest point of the river which is of a gun's reach." (Detroit Historical Museum.)

Focused on military control of the river, Cadillac reminded his superiors in France that the straits were navigable to 100-gun vessels and by positioning it on the narrowest point of the river no one could pass by day without being observed. Concerned with protecting the Native American fur trade, he noted that traders abuse Native Americans but not under the "bastions of the fort." Cadillac suggested 12 companies to garrison the fortifications. (Detroit Historical Museum.)

The French and Indian War resulted in the British conquest of Canada and Detroit surrendered to Maj. Robert Rogers and his Majesty's Rangers in 1760. The fort was garrisoned by 120 officers and men. During the American Revolution, the British used Detroit as a staging area for raids against American settlers. In response, plans were put before the Continental Congress to capture the fort at Detroit. (Burton Collection.)

In 1778, George Rogers Clark's successful assault on the British garrison at Vincennes created panic for the fort at Detroit. It was clear the old walls of Fort Pontchartrain would not withstand a siege. A second fort was constructed and named Fort Lernoult for its commander. War never came to Detroit, and though it was designated American territory in the treaty of 1783, the British forces did not evacuate the fort. (Detroit Historical Museum.)

Detroit remained in British hands until the defeat of their Native American allies at the Battle of Fallen Timbers. Gen. Anthony Wayne, commander of the victorious American Legion, next moved on Detroit's Fort Lernoult, demanding its surrender. The British complied and on July 11, 1796, the flag of the United States, which included 15 stars and stripes, was raised over Detroit for the first time. Fort Lernoult was renamed Fort Shelby. (Detroit Historical Museum.)

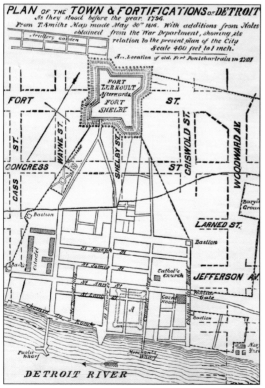

During the War of 1812, Gen. William Hull surrendered Detroit to British forces without providing any resistance. For his actions at Detroit, Hull was court-martialed but spared execution by Pres. James Madison. The British later abandoned Detroit and American troops reoccupied Fort Shelby. The inability of the army to resupply it led to shortages of food and medicine and an epidemic broke out. As many as 700 soldiers died as a result. The surrender of Detroit during the War of 1812 was a humiliating loss for the United States in its war with Britain. An entire army was lost and the planned invasion of Canada had to be abandoned as a result. The memory of this defeat coming from British troops stationed across the Detroit River at Fort Malden would play a major role in the decision to build Fort Wayne. (Detroit Historical Museum.)

The Patriot War of 1837–1838, resulted from actions by residents of Canada and the United States who were living in Canada. The "patriots," as they called themselves, intended to make the Canadian peninsula between Michigan and the Niagara region part of the United States. Canadian forces led by Gen. Hugh Brady suppressed this rebellion against British authority. The British military response to this threat raised tensions along the Detroit River. (Detroit Historical Museum.)

Pres. Martin Van Buren was in office less than a year when the Patriot War broke out. A border raid in New York by Canadian militia leading to an American's death, a retaliatory burning of a Canadian vessel, and American support for the rebels along the Detroit River could have easily led to a third war with Great Britain. Van Buren responded to these provocations by ordering two proclamations of neutrality. (NARA.)

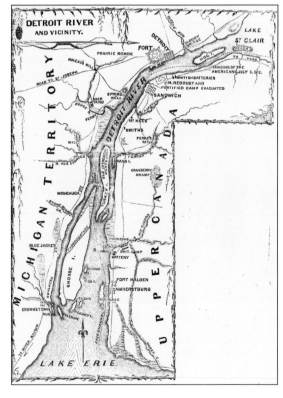

After the War of 1812, Fort Shelby was allowed to decay. In 1826, it was sold to the City of Detroit, the stockade pickets were sold at auction, and the fort was demolished. It would play no role when the army returned to Detroit in the future. Today all that remains of Fort Shelby is a historical marker on the corner of Fort and Shelby Streets in downtown Detroit. (Detroit Historical Museum.)

Following American independence, the British constructed Fort Amherstburg in Ontario at the mouth of the Detroit River. It was the headquarters for British forces in the area during the War of 1812. After the war, Fort Malden was rebuilt. The strengthening of this fort in 1838 and its role as a military center in the Patriot War led American military leaders to conclude a corresponding fort was required at Detroit. (Detroit Historical Museum.)

Tensions mounted between the United States and Great Britain as armed supporters of the patriots attempted to capture arsenals and raided Canada. Prior to the construction of Fort Wayne, the U.S. Army regarrisoned Detroit using rented quarters on the lower east-side of town. These quarters, the post at Detroit, became the Detroit Barracks. In Washington, D.C., Gen. Winfield Scott and his officers began developing a defensive system for the nation's northern boundary. (Detroit Historical Museum.)

GRANT, U.S.

ULYSSES S. GRANT.
LIEUTENANT GENERAL, U. S. A.

A young lieutenant, Ulysses Grant, served in Detroit from 1849 to 1851, and probably toured the new fort on the river. Construction of Fort Wayne was complete but the garrison remained in the Detroit Barracks. Grant wrote in his personal memoirs, "I was ordered to Detroit, Michigan, where two years were spent with but few . . . incidents." In 1851 the 4th Infantry and Grant were transferred to Sackett's Harbor, New York. (Library of Congress.)

Most army officers assigned to Detroit lived in hotels, but Grant, with a wife and child, purchased a two-story Greek Revival home for his residence. He was a well-known figure in the city, participating in horse racing, a sport popular in the period. Later the home he lived in was moved to the Michigan State Fairgrounds. It is preserved as a monument to the man and his accomplishments. (Detroit Historical Museum.)

Three

BUILDING FORT WAYNE

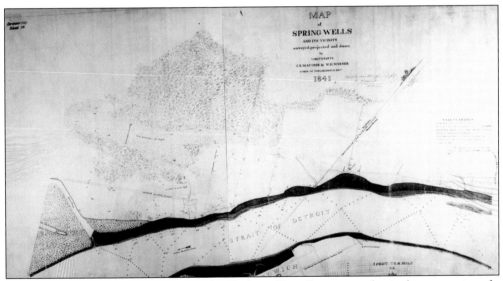

In accordance with the army's Great Lakes Defense Plan, Congress authorized construction of a new fort at Detroit on August 4, 1841. The forts envisaged in the plan were not as sophisticated as the seacoast defenses of the period. Fort Wayne was designed to assist ground force operations, to control the Detroit River, and protect the city of Detroit. The fort's garrison was not capable of resisting a protracted siege. The site selected for the Detroit fort was three miles west of the city in Springwells Township. The government purchased 96 acres for a military reservation on the river based on a survey of the Detroit River that was conducted in 1840 by Lt. John Macomb of the Army Corps of Topographical Engineers. Macomb, a Detroit native and graduate of West Point, was the future brother-in-law to Capt. Montgomery Meigs who superintended construction of Fort Wayne. (Detroit Historical Museum.)

Montgomery Meigs, an engineering officer, designed and superintended the construction of Fort Wayne. An 1836 West Point graduate, he lived in Detroit from 1843 to 1851 during the fort's construction. During the Civil War, he served as quartermaster general for the Union Army. In 1864, Meigs ordered 26 dead Union soldiers, taken from an army morgue, to be buried near Gen. Robert E. Lee's mansion, creating the Arlington National Cemetery. (NARA.)

This building was the engineering office during construction of the star fort, and during the Civil War it was Gen. John C. Robinson's headquarters. From this office, Meigs designed and supervised the fort's construction. Assisting him was Lt. John Newton, a Virginian who remained with the Union during the Civil War. After becoming a general, Newton helped construct the Washington defenses and led a corps at the Battle of Gettysburg during Pickett's Charge. (Detroit Historical Museum.)

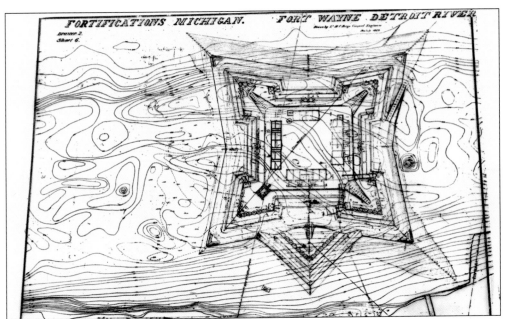

Planned as a square bastioned fort, the design was based on the art of fortification developed by the French military engineer, Sebastian Vauban, and modified by the teachings of the American military theorist Dennis Hart Mahan. Vauban's designs had dominated western military construction for more than 200 years. The various elements of his fortifications were designed to force attackers to face a succession of obstacles in trying to gain entry. (Detroit Historical Museum.)

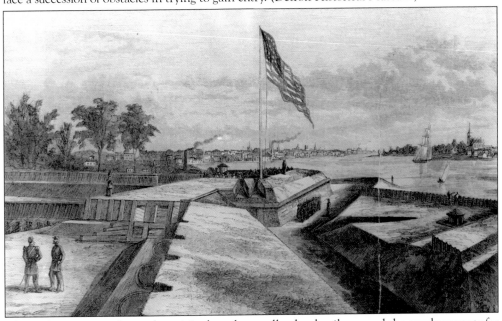

This 1861 engraving shows the original earthen walls, the demilune, and the emplacements for cannon. The cedar logs for facing the scarp came from Kellys Island in Lake Erie and the gun embrasures were made of Michigan oak. The fort, similar to all northern chain forts, was not designed to resist a long siege. The long logistical tail of any attacking forces meant the fort need only withstand a limited duration attack. (Detroit Historical Museum.)

Limestone for the fort and barracks was quarried on Kellys Island in Lake Erie. The island is composed of limestone bedrock. Glacial striations in the bedrock can still be viewed in areas not previously quarried. In 1863, revisions to the fort replaced the earthen walls with brick purchased locally from Springwells and Detroit-area suppliers of brick and tile. Brick was also used for additions to the limestone barracks. (Detroit Historical Museum.)

In 1849, War Department Order No. 6 named the fort for Revolutionary War hero Gen. Anthony Wayne. He was popularly known as "Mad" Anthony Wayne, probably for his impetuous behavior in combat. Called the "chief who never sleeps" by his Native American foes, he commanded the American Legion that defeated them at the Battle of Fallen Timbers near present-day Toledo in 1794, effectively ending British power on American soil. (NARA.)

When closed and bolted, these massive wooden gates provided a substantial obstacle to attackers. The vertical, horizontal, and diagonal arrangement of Michigan oak planks was reinforced with wrought iron bands on the exterior and crossbeams on the interior. An iron bar rotated to lock the doors. The smaller door, called a "wickette gate," allowed the garrison entry without having to open the main gate. (Detroit Historical Museum.)

The sally port is a heavily fortified gateway from which the garrison can rush out, strike attacking forces, and quickly return to the safety of the fort's interior. The sally port, as a feature of defensive works, can be dated back to the period of the Crusades. At Fort Wayne there was only one sally port entrance. It is located in the southeast bastion. (Detroit Historical Museum.)

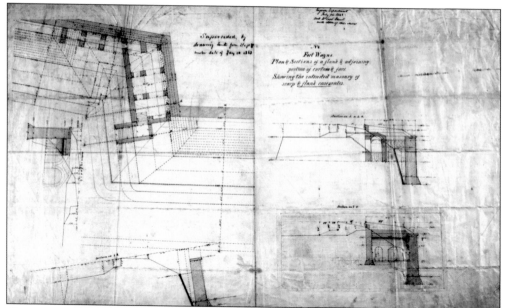

The casemate is a system of artillery emplacements in which a battery of guns is mounted side-by-side in a protected room. The casemates in the bastions of the star fort are situated so that there is no dead ground along the walls. Dead ground is the area where the defender's fire cannot reach. The casemates at Fort Wayne included a room to store ammunition and loopholes for infantry fire. (Detroit Historical Museum.)

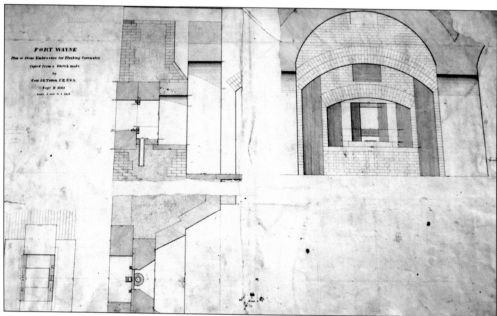

Casemates at the fort follow the design developed by the principal American fortress engineer of the period, Col. Joseph Totten. One innovation was the Totten embrasure. In this design, the cannon pivoted about a pintle socket forward in the embrasure, or gun opening. This permitted both a smaller opening and a wide field of fire. When the gun was being loaded iron doors were closed to protect the gun crew from hostile fire. (Detroit Historical Museum.)

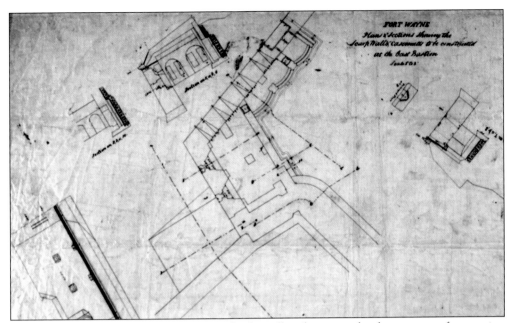

The casemates were designed for housing flank artillery howitzers for the purpose of protecting the fort itself. The guns would be mounted on swiveling wooden carriages within the casemate to provide fire along the exterior walls of the fort. Recoil of the guns was absorbed by the chassis's slope and the friction of the carriage wheels. The wheels were used to return the gun to its firing position after loading. (Detroit Historical Museum.)

The powder magazine stored ammunition for the fort's artillery. Its brick barrel vaulted ceiling is less robust than the thick walls allowing the force of an accidental detonation to escape skyward. The arched ceiling protects against penetration from high trajectory mortars. A major problem faced by military architects resulted from the need to safely store ammunition below ground while making it accessible to gun crews high on the parapets. (Detroit Historical Museum.)

A stone lining, or revetment, surrounds the powder magazine. It is composed of limestone blocks two feet thick, backed by another two feet of rubble stone. The stone rubble provides drainage for the revetment. A gap of three feet separates the revetment and the walls of the powder magazine. The revetment is designed to prevent erosion of the upper terreplein roadway and protect the scarp from the effects of an explosion in the powder magazine. (Detroit Historical Museum.)

This 1852 sketch shows the completed soldiers' barracks. The barracks, located adjacent and parallel to southwest curtain, are three and a half stories high and constructed of limestone and brick. The barracks are sectioned into five bays. Interior walls and ceilings are plastered. The flooring on the first floor is brick paving while the remaining floors are wood over masonry vaults except for the fireplace hearths and the edges of the rooms. (Detroit Historical Museum.)

The troop barracks constructed between 1842 and 1849 is considered the best example of Federal-style architecture outside the seaboard states. The exterior walls are constructed of ashlars, rough-hewn blocks of limestone. Its interior is composed of five adjacent, but independent sections for housing the fort's garrison. Each section contained a ground floor mess hall (kitchen, pantry, and dining area), two floors of barracks rooms, and an attic. (Detroit Historical Museum.)

Scattered in the foreground are limestone fragments. Limestone from Kellys Island, located downriver from the fort in Lake Erie, was used to construct the barracks, powder magazine, and pave the passages of the sally port and postern in the fort. The impressive soldiers' barracks are constructed of limestone masonry laid with cut and dressed limestone quoined at the corners to extend the height of the walls. (Detroit Historical Museum.)

This Civil War–period photograph of Union infantry shows the wooden revetment that once lined the outside of the star fort. The revetment was designed to prevent the earthen banks from collapsing by facing and reinforcing them with wood or stone walls keyed into the earth. At Fort Wayne, wood was used and beams can be seen keyed above the planked walls. (Burton Collection.)

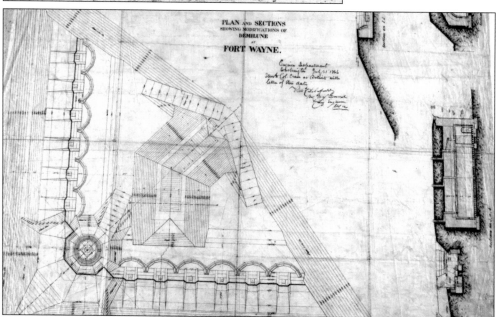

The army chief engineer, Brigadier General Delafield, took a direct interest in Fort Wayne and sent plans for modifications to the demilune in 1863. The demilune is the outwork located on the riverfront. It serves as the water battery. It was arranged to hold 12 seacoast guns, 10-inch smooth bore Rodmans along the faces of the work, and a 15-inch Rodman at the salient, mounted on barbette carriages. (Detroit Historical Museum.)

The demilune is a freestanding, triangular fortification with a concave rear face located in front of a Vauban design fort. This fortification provides the defending force with the ability to provide artillery fire over a wider area of approach from the river. A separate powder magazine located beneath the demilune provided the gun crews with ready access to ammunition resupply. (Detroit Historical Museum.)

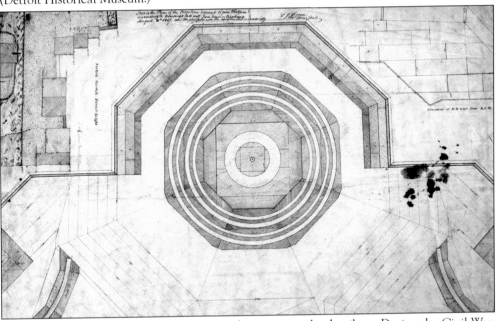

Drawings from 1863 show a 15-inch gun emplacement on the demilune. During the Civil War, 15-inch Rodman guns were replacing older cannons on third system forts. With a 50-pound charge, this rifled gun fired a 330-pound projectile to a maximum range of 4,680 yards. It is not known if guns were in place during the war, but later reports show no armament mounted on the fort's walls. (Detroit Historical Museum.)

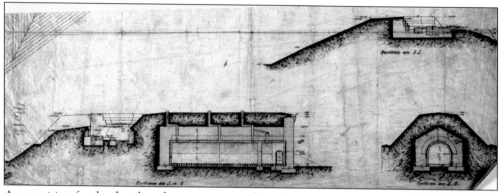

Ammunition for the demilune battery was stored in a large traverse magazine built in the gorge of the demilune. The magazine is located in the center of the demilune and to the rear of the gun platforms. Four ducts in the crown of the arched ceiling provide ventilation for the magazine that is protected with 13 feet of earth covering making it bombproof. (Detroit Historical Museum.)

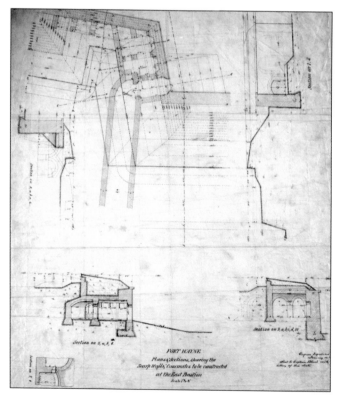

The east bastion is the projection at the east angle of the enclosure. It is unique to the other bastions in its design to accommodate internal passages for the sally port and postern. The passageways reduce the number of flanking guns. Access to the terreplein of the bastion is by a stone paved ramp between the revetments supporting the gorge. The terreplein is level with the terrepleins of the adjacent curtains. (Detroit Historical Museum.)

34

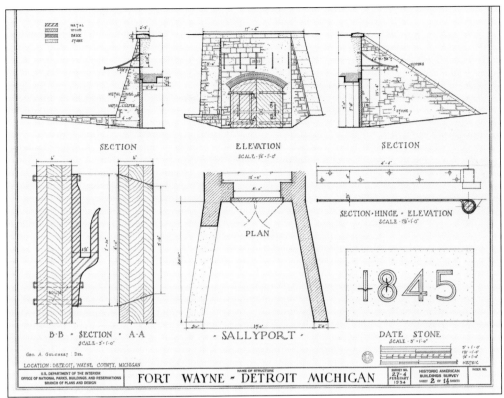

The east sally port was the main entry to the fort. A segmentally arched and vaulted passage 10 feet wide, it makes a 90-degree turn to the right side of the east bastion. The sally port contains three sets of heavily timbered doors that conform to the arches. Two sets of doors control access to the sally port; the third encloses a four-foot doorway to the flank casemate. (Detroit Historical Museum.)

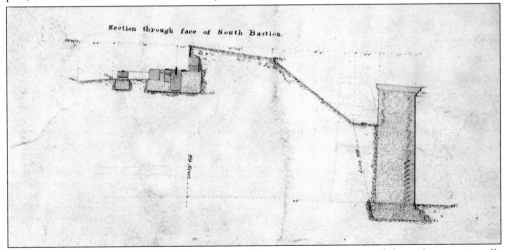

The south bastion is similar to the east, except the casemates are accessed through two stairwells on the banquette of the flanks. The stairwells were covered by wood-framed penthouses covered in canvas. Casemates in the south bastion have additional flank howitzers. The bastion casemates each had their own powder magazine that featured a "weak" wall designed to blow out into the ditch in the event the powder magazine exploded. (Detroit Historical Museum.)

The batteries were designed for a 10-inch smooth bore cannon mounted "en barbette," meaning to fire over the parapet. The above image from the defenses of Washington, D.C., demonstrates the type of mounting envisaged at Fort Wayne. Some research indicates the fort's cannons were declared obsolete before the Civil War and removed. Army reports for the 1870s and 1880s show no cannons mounted at Fort Wayne. (NARA.)

Water collected from the barracks downspouts ran through ceramic drain pipes along the barrack's foundation into a large underground masonry cistern. This tank served as an emergency water supply in case the fort was besieged. Major General Cram reported that it was cleaned in 1869. This cleaning limited the finds by Wayne State University archeologist Gordon Grosscup's 1978 team to materials from a later date. (Detroit Historical Museum.)

Disease was the greatest killer in armies of the 1800s. Typhoid, a human pathogen occurring when food or water is contaminated by feces, was of particular concern to commanders. Poor locating of latrines with respect to kitchens contributed to high rates of disease in military units. At Fort Wayne early latrines were located in a separate building from the barracks where the troops lived and prepared their meals. (Detroit Historical Museum.)

It is conservatively estimated that the Union and Confederate Armies used over a million horses during the American Civil War. The stationing of field artillery units, officer's mounts, and quartermaster requirements at Fort Wayne required a sizeable stock of hay and feed to be available to supply the horses and mules used by the garrison. This hay barn would have kept food for the animals of the garrison. (Detroit Historical Museum.)

The old parade field in front of officer's row was a quarter of the size it is today before improvements were made adding 20 acres to the fort by filling in areas of the swamp by the river bank. The dredging of the wetlands began between 1879 and 1881, according to the memory of Theodore Lentz, a steward at the Fort Wayne Hospital during that period, and continued until 1896. (Detroit Historical Museum.)

This main gate at Fort Wayne, in use during the 1880s, opened to Springwells Township, which later became part of the city of Detroit. Based on the 1880 census, this was a lower-middle-class community. Local factories produced rail cars, furnaces, organs, lumber, glass, matches, tobacco, and stoves. The township had two justices of the peace but no policeman, and there was only one clergyman, a Roman Catholic priest. (Detroit Historical Museum.)

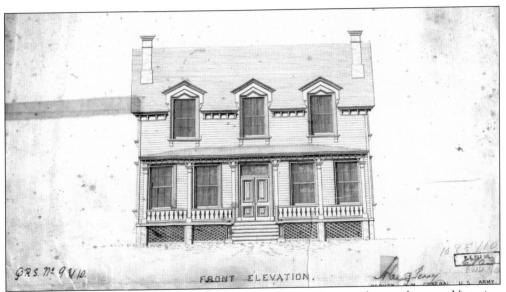

Built in 1880 to replace the Civil War vintage commander's residence, the new Victorian cottage–style residence provided large high-ceilinged rooms for the regiment's commander and his family. The first floor featured a double parlor, dining room, kitchen, and a downstairs bedroom. The second floor had four family bedrooms, an indoor bathroom, and a bedroom in the back for the household servant. There were many complaints that the house was cold and drafty in the winter, but the standard design was thought suitable for any climate. (Detroit Historical Museum.)

During the years 1890–1910, four brick barracks were constructed east of the star fort. The new buildings were constructed using standardized plans developed by the Quartermaster Division at Army Headquarters in Washington, D.C. They each were capable of housing two companies of soldiers. By the time they were built, the old barracks had become substandard for housing troops. The new buildings featured modern amenities such as electric lighting, indoor plumbing, and central steam heating (Detroit Historical Museum.)

The guardhouse constructed in 1889 is modeled on the frame Civil War–era building it replaced. The facility includes individual cells for serious offenders and communal cells for Article 15-level offenses. Other rooms had space for the part of the daily guard not on duty, an office for the sergeant of the guard, and a washroom. Behind the guardhouse is a stockade exercise area for the prisoners. (Detroit Historical Museum.)

The census for the period lists 278 men, women, and children living at Fort Wayne. The entire fort was considered as one residence. The record does not provide ranks for the residents, but it begins with the commanding officer and among the first 18 names, all married, are two surgeons, which is an indication that these were the fort's officers who lived in the buildings of officer's row. (Detroit Historical Museum.)

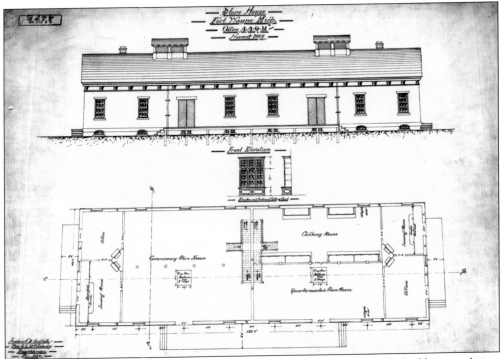

The Quartermaster Corps is the U.S. Army's oldest logistics branch, established by a resolution of the Continental Congress in June 1775. At the time this storehouse was constructed in 1890, the quartermaster was responsible for military transportation, clothing, and construction materials. In storehouses like this one, the quartermaster maintained stocks of clothing, tools, construction materials, and rations. The quartermaster performed his duties from offices in the storehouse. (Detroit Historical Museum.)

The brick hospital constructed in 1890 included offices and examining rooms for physicians and wards for the patients. Before the hospital it replaced was remodeled, the hospital at Fort Wayne was considered insufficient. Post Surgeon Irwin wrote of it that "buildings used for the accommodation of the sick at this post were not only inadequate, but in many particulars were defective and unsuitable for the use of invalids." (Detroit Historical Museum.)

In 1898, the hospital was expanded to include an isolation ward and an east wing in addition to the original central two and a half story pavilion. Each wing of the hospital was designed to accommodate 12 patients and was equipped with verandas for all invalid soldiers to enjoy recovering in fresh air. The building featured classical architectural elements like the original soldiers' barracks in the star fort. (Detroit Historical Museum.)

In 1903, the cedar logs that remained as revetments for the various slopes in the star fort were removed. The post carpenter, George Morrill, who worked in the carpenter shop shown, recalled that you could smell the "woodsy" aroma of the decaying logs as much as two or three blocks distant from the fort during this modification. (Detroit Historical Museum.)

In 1905, a new guardhouse was constructed adjacent to the fort's main gate. The broad overhang on the porch protected the guard from inclement weather during the daily inspection known as guard mount. Inside, the building contained an office for the sergeant of the guard, a central room for housing the daily guard detail, and cells for prisoners. Today the facility supports the fort's private security service. (Detroit Historical Museum.)

The last stables at Fort Wayne were built in 1908. There were no longer field artillery units assigned to the post by that time and the stables were constructed exclusively for the animals that were needed to haul food and other supplies required to keep the fort operating. Period photographs show carriages on officer's row, and some of the carriage horses may have been stabled here. (Detroit Historical Museum.)

Fort Wayne facilities were continually evolving as new technology changed the army. The garages shown here in front of the star fort resulted from changes in transportation from the horse and carriage to the automobile, for which automobile entrepreneurs living in Detroit were largely responsible. These garages served officers living in the adjacent bachelor officer quarters constructed in 1904. (Detroit Historical Museum.)

Originally the only entrance to the fort was through the sally port in the East Bastion. It was not until 1938 that the triple arched entrance was constructed as shown in this World War II photograph. Designed originally for pedestrian and vehicular traffic the arches themselves were later removed to accommodate larger military vehicles. (Detroit Historical Museum.)

Four

CIVIL WAR YEARS

In his second inaugural address, Abraham Lincoln reminded the nation, "but one of them would make war rather than let the nation survive, and the other would accept war rather than let it perish, and the war came." Civil War brought massive change to the unmanned, unarmed fort at Detroit. Thousands of soldiers passed through heading for battlefields south and its earthen fortifications would be replaced by brick and concrete walls. (NARA.)

The shot furnace was completed in 1847. The furnace heated non-explosive cannonballs for use against wooden hulled warships where it could start a fire in the wood, tarred cordage, canvas sails, gunpowder, and so on. A typical furnace in the 1800s cost about $300. Three men operated a shot furnace; one maintained the fire and loaded cold cannonballs, a second unloaded the hot projectiles, and the third cleaned them. (Burton Collection.)

Capt. Alfred Gibbs, an 1846 graduate of West Point, commanded the United States 3rd Cavalry, the first regular army unit to occupy the fort. Gibbs and two companies of his regiment served their paroles at Fort Wayne, having been captured early in 1861 by Confederate forces in the west. Wounded during the Mexican and Indian Wars, he rose to the rank of major general of cavalry during the Civil War. (Library of Congress Prints and Photographs Collection.)

The intensive training provided to volunteers at Fort Wayne resulted in orders issued in 1861 by the War Department designating it a "camp of instruction." These soldiers are being trained to form an infantry square. The square, an early infantry tactic used against cavalry was described by Plutarch as a Roman formation. A battalion was normally the smallest force to drill in forming a square. It was used throughout the 19th century. (Burton Collection.)

The Coldwater Cadets were among the first Michigan troops stationed at Fort Wayne. An element of the 1st Michigan Infantry Regiment, it was mustered into federal service in May 1861. They joined the Army of the Potomac, fighting at the first Battle of Bull Run. Returning to Michigan, the regiment reorganized and returned to fight the major battles in the east and was at Appomattox when Gen. Robert E. Lee surrendered. (Detroit Historical Museum.)

Weapons for the 1st Michigan Infantry Regiment training at Fort Wayne in June 1861 were purchased through public subscription. In the early days of the war some infantry units were provided cannons. The shortage of available armament resulted in weapons of varying types and vintage being provided to the units. The Model 1841, six-pounder cannons, were considered obsolete though many saw service particularly in Confederate artillery units. (Detroit Historical Museum.)

The 1st Michigan Infantry is shown here in formation in Detroit. In May 1861, only one month after it had been authorized by the governor, the regiment of 780 strong, under the command of Col. O. B. Wilcox, marched east becoming the first of the western regiments to arrive in Washington to defend the nation's capital. Before leaving Detroit, the regiment received its banners in a ceremony at Campus Martius. (Detroit Historical Museum.)

From the army's beginning, regular infantry regiments carried colors. Regiments did not carry the national flag. No single unit could carry the national standard into battle. If the colors were lost in battle, the regiment's honor was lost. A soldier capturing enemy colors or saving his unit's colors was recognized. Volunteer regiments received their colors in local ceremonies. The 1st Michigan Infantry Regiment is shown receiving its colors in downtown Detroit. (Detroit Historical Museum.)

Artillery gun crews trained at Fort Wayne during the Civil War. Early in the war, artillery was part of some infantry regiments but soon all field guns were grouped in batteries. Guns were pulled by six horses hooked to a limber that carried an ammunition chest for the piece. Each piece had its own caisson carrying three additional ammunition chests. A battery of six guns was commanded by a captain. (Detroit Historical Museum.)

Soldiers of the Detroit garrison billeted in the Detroit Barracks. Fort Wayne was not garrisoned until 1861 when companies of the 3rd United States Cavalry occupied the post. During the Civil War, the post was filled beyond capacity as volunteers mustered and trained for war. The barracks could not house the numbers arriving. Tents were used to shelter volunteers and the steamboat *Mississippi* docked at the fort to quarter soldiers. (Detroit Historical Museum.)

Officer housing was originally built in the star fort opposite the soldiers' barracks. The masonry and wood homes burned prior to the Civil War and were not rebuilt. Subsequently a row of officer homes was constructed west of the fortifications. These homes for officers and their families were replaced during the 1880s. Families living here were part of the permanent garrison with families of regiments being trained remaining at home. (Detroit Historical Museum.)

The post surgeon described the Civil War guardhouse (center): "The guard-house is on the southwest corner of the new parade ground, outside the fortifications, and is a strongly constructed frame building, 54' long by 30'. It is divided into the guardroom . . . two prison rooms are heavily barred with close iron gratings. The heating is afforded by a large No. 10 wood stove placed in the center of the guard room." (Detroit Historical Museum.)

In his 1870 report, Surgeon Irwin described these as, "buildings situated outside of the defensive works, appear to have been constructed with a view to meeting the temporary wants of the garrison until such times as . . . other buildings suitable for a permanent stronghold could be furnished . . . little has been done . . . improving the quarters, grounds, drainage . . . artillery stables have been occupied temporarily as commissary and quartermaster's store room." (Detroit Historical Museum.)

Asa Sprague was commissioned a lieutenant in the 24th Michigan Infantry and trained at Fort Wayne during the Civil War serving with the Army of the Potomac. With his regiment, Sprague fought at the Battle of Gettysburg and was captured during the fighting. He died a prisoner of war at Charleston, South Carolina, in the 1863. (Detroit Historical Museum.)

This Civil War image appears to be of a riverside washhouse. If this was its function, it had been removed by 1870 when Surgeon Irwin reported, "There is no general laundry at the post, the washing of the command being done by the laundresses at their quarters." Enlisted men's wives continued washing at the river as evidenced by the name Soapsuds Row that was given to their small frame houses. (Burton Collection.)

This Civil War photograph of an infantry company was taken before the 1863 modifications. Visible over the wood fence are the ruins of the officers' quarters that burned in 1850. Nearly 13,000 cubic feet of oak logs, impregnated with mercuric chloride to retard decay, were used to build the revetments of the scarp, some of which can be seen behind the soldiers. Cedar was used for the breast height wall. (Burton Collection.)

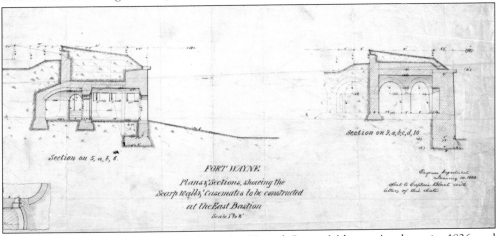

Thomas Jefferson Cram graduated from the United States Military Academy in 1826 and remained as assistant professor of mathematics and of natural and experimental philosophy. In 1855, he became chief topographical engineer, in the Department of the Pacific. He was brevetted brigadier-general for service during the Civil War. After the war he superintended new construction at Fort Wayne and served on engineering boards studying improvements to Great Lakes' harbors until retiring in 1869. The general plan of the fort remained the same but the decaying old cedar log scarp was removed and replaced with a brick and concrete wall. The wall is 22 feet high, and seven and a half feet thick. The facing of the wall is made of brick and measures 18 inches thick. The brick has a backing of six feet of concrete. (Detroit Historical Museum.)

Under the supervision of Thomas Jefferson Cram, reconstruction of Fort Wayne began in 1863 during the some of the most intense fighting of the Civil War. In addition to the wall, the ramps to the fort were paved with stone, outer gates of the posterns constructed and gun emplacements for the fort's 64 cannons were repaired. (Detroit Historical Museum.)

This Civil War photograph of the east bastion shows modifications to the breast high wall. The wall of limestone and Amherst sandstone masonry retains the sandy soil of the parapet. The stone is secured with iron tie-bars. Three guns sit in the foreground. On the left is a field artillery Parrot Gun; in the middle is a muzzle-loading rifled steel U.S. Navy 12-pounder; at right is a truck mounted siege gun. (Burton Collection.)

Five

GARRISON LIFE

The original limestone troop barracks were constructed with no accommodation for sanitary facilities. It was determined that outside facilities were inadequate to serve great numbers of troops. To remedy this, five brick additions were built on the rear of the building in 1861 for the large numbers of troops living in the barracks during the Civil War. The red brick additions housed both washrooms and kitchens. (Detroit Historical Museum.)

Though Fort Wayne was designed to be a riverside artillery post, the first troops to garrison the fort were Companies B and F of the 3rd United States Cavalry commanded by Capt. Alfred Gibbs. The street on the post in front of the officers' quarters facing the parade field is named in his honor. (Detroit Historical Museum.)

Life on Michigan garrison posts may have lacked combat, but discontent sometimes arose. In 1829 and 1830, a young infantry lieutenant at Fort Gratiot, later a sub post of Fort Wayne, noted in his diary two threats against his life by enlisted men. He took them seriously since someone had recently killed a sergeant. A soldier did wound the young officer in August 1830, but this was apparently an accident. (Detroit Historical Museum.)

56

The barracks, built in 1851, was described in a report by Surgeon Irwin as follows. "The quarters were evidently designed and finished with accommodation of a battalion of five small companies of troops. The building is divided into five equal divisions, which are in turn sub-divided into halls, dormitories, dining rooms, etc. . . . These quarters are exceptionally good and well adapted for troops serving in this latitude." (Detroit Historical Museum.)

In 1870, Surgeon Irwin described the earlier officers' quarters as "two story frame cottages, built in a somewhat cheap tenement style . . . built to face east and the river . . . Owing to the frail nature of the material used in their construction . . . they are intensely cold and uncomfortable during the winter season. Their position is a very bad one, and they are necessarily crowded . . . privies are inconveniently located within a few feet of the dining room doors." (Detroit Historical Museum.)

In the 1870s, a pass was required for soldiers to go beyond the ditch of the star fort. When they could obtain that pass, the soldiers would cross Jefferson Avenue and visit Ratigan's Grocery located directly in front of the fort's main gate. Their destination was often the Sample Room, a tavern with beer priced at 5¢ a glass and bar liquor at 10¢ for three ounces. (Detroit Historical Museum.)

This brick building that last housed Ratigan's Grocery served other purposes once the fort's garrison used its new found mobility to find wide ranging locations in Detroit to frequent. For a period after the fort ended its military usefulness, the building served as a church. After standing vacant for many years, in 2005 the old structure was torn down to make room for a parking lot to store commercial vehicles. (Detroit Historical Museum.)

The Post Bakery was described by Surgeon Irwin as being "a suitable frame building, 30 feet by 18, with brick ovens capable of baking for 1,000 men. The building is divided into a capacious well-ventilated work-room, store room, and sleeping apartment for the baker." This photograph of the bakery, taken about 1870, includes a sergeant with his bicycle and son visiting the baker. (Detroit Historical Museum.)

This 1883 drawing of the Detroit River from the Fort Wayne parade field would appear to represent a well-landscaped park rather than a military installation. The piers that permitted shipping to dock at the fort can be seen in the background. Perhaps mindful of the river, the commander of the 26th Infantry Regiment ordered that all soldiers learn to swim. Lessons were given in the Detroit YMCA swimming pool. (Detroit Historical Museum.)

Fire was a danger in frame homes, like this one for noncommissioned officers, heated by fireplaces and later wood burning stoves. The fire buckets hanging on the porch were kept filled with water. The post guard was instructed, "In case of fire . . . call 'Fire No __' adding the number of his post; if possible he will extinguish the fire himself." When fire occurred in the stables, guards raised the alarm then moved the horses to safety. (Detroit Historical Museum.)

This is a view of officer's housing in the 1880s. The homes in this photograph still have the shutters and old-style porches that would disappear during the fort's reconstruction period. The home of the fort's commanding officer is to the right. From 1884 to 1890 this was the home of Col. Henry M. Black, commanding officer of the Fort Wayne garrison, the 23rd Infantry Regiment. (Detroit Historical Museum.)

This room, furnished in the style of the 1880s, was the personal study of the commanding officer. Col. Henry B. Clitz, commander of the 10th Infantry Regiment during the 1879–1884 period, was a favorite of Detroit society. When he retired from the army, Clitz settled in Detroit on Woodward Avenue. He left the city unexpectedly and was last reported to have been seen near Niagara Falls. (Detroit Historical Museum.)

The birth of American football is attributed to a meeting between college representatives from Harvard, Columbia, Princeton, and Yale that took place in November 1876 in Springfield, Massachusetts. Twenty-one years after what became known as the Massasoit Convention which set standard rules for the sport, members of the 19th Infantry Regiment football team posed at Fort Wayne in their uniforms for this photograph. (Detroit Historical Museum.)

The fort's parade ground, located between housing on officer's row and the Detroit River, was constantly being expanded. This open area served as a field for artillery and infantry drill, military parades and inspections, athletic competition, and picnics. Covered pavilions were erected along the Gibbs Street edge of the parade ground to shelter the military bands giving concerts to the families at the fort and visitors from Detroit. (Detroit Historical Museum.)

The houses located on officer's row served varied functions at different times in the post's history. The buildings were originally intended to serve as housing for company and field grade commissioned officers assigned to the fort. They performed that function for many decades. As the needs of the post changed, some housing was converted to administrative offices, an officer's club, and a school for the army's chaplain corps. (Detroit Historical Museum.)

Expansion of post facilities in 1897 caused removal of the military cemetery located at the west end of the fort. The graves of soldiers and their families were moved to Detroit's Woodmere Cemetery located on West Fort Street. Life was tenuous for army wives and children. One of the gravestones reads in part, "Born at Fort Logan. Colorado. January 30, 1896—Died at Fort Wayne January 26, 1899." (Detroit Historical Museum.)

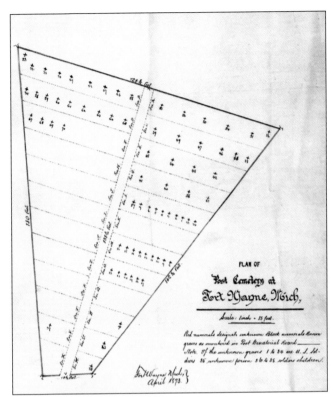

The original design of the star fort provided for exits only at the Southeast Bastion where a tunnel led to the sally port exit and an adjacent tunnel provided access to a postern exiting to the river demilune battery and powder magazine. The bridge shown in the foreground of this photograph later provided a way for occupants of the barracks to cross over the western curtain wall. (Detroit Historical Museum.)

Around 1900, Fort Wayne's soldiers trained much as soldiers do today. The troops engaged in company and battalion drills, patrols, bayonet practice, advance and rear guard drills, learned to entrench, attack outposts, conduct marches, and participated in daily calisthenics. Newspapers of the period reported a common exercise was the "shelter tent drill" involving 300 troops equipped with knapsacks. (Detroit Historical Museum.)

The presence of soldiers' families, particularly that of children seems to have relaxed the strict military discipline of earlier periods. Here children climb on a Spanish American War–era artillery piece while their fathers lounge against its wheel. The sign in front of it ordering Do Not Climb on the Gun is ignored with impunity as the photograph is made. (Detroit Historical Museum.)

From its earliest occupation by military forces during the 1830s Black Hawk War, the site of Fort Wayne sent troops to fight in far off battlefields. Here units depart from the city of Detroit to fight in the Spanish American War of 1898. Photographs from soldiers of the 2nd Infantry Regiment show their comrades in the Philippines indicating that individuals returned to the fort at the end of the war. (Detroit Historical Museum.)

In the last three decades of the 19th century, 2,100 officers and 25,000 men occupied 200 posts including these at Fort Wayne. From the time of the War of 1812 until 1857, pay remained the same. A second lieutenant's $25 monthly salary was not lucrative. Long-serving officers had limited chances for promotion. In January 1861, the commander of the 4th Infantry was William Whistler. With 60 years service he had commanded the regiment since 1845. (Detroit Historical Museum.)

These sergeants posing in front of the barracks around 1898 were assigned to the 2nd Infantry Regiment. The regiment had a long history and was nearly as old as the nation. The assignment of the regiment to the fort at Detroit was appropriate, as it was elements of the 2nd Infantry that had originally taken possession of Detroit for the United States from the British in 1796. (Detroit Historical Museum.)

The tour of guard duty lasted 24 hours. Before being posted, the guard was inspected. The commander of the guard, the officer of the day, the commanding officer, and all those with authority over the commanding officer were entitled to inspect the guard. The commander of the guard also inspected the guardhouse to see that it was clean and that nothing not pertaining to the guard was present. (Detroit Historical Museum.)

These noncommissioned officers were assigned to Company B, 19th Infantry Regiment that was stationed at Fort Wayne from May 1890 until October 1898. Soldiers of the regiment manned the sub posts controlled by the fort as well. The regiment saw action during the Spanish American War fighting in the Philippines. A noncommissioned officer controls a unit as opposed to command, a term applying to commissioned officers only. (Detroit Historical Museum.)

Mounted on the Southeast Bastion facing the Detroit River is a three-inch Ordnance Rifle. The breast height wall was lowered here to allow the "sunset gun" to project over the wall. The gun fired saluting the national colors being lowered at sunset. By tradition it also fired salutes to warships passing on the river. The gun was removed by the army before the fort was given to the historical museum. (Burton Collection.)

During World War I the army found that sports helped to promote and maintain military efficiency and morale. Following World War II, the army chief of special services offered a program of recreational athletics that included boxing, football, baseball, softball, tennis, golf, track, field, badminton, bowling, and swimming. On a corner of the parade field at Fort Wayne a baseball diamond has been laid out for ball playing. (Detroit Historical Museum.)

The guardhouse is an important center of military activity. This 1905 facility housed prisoners and the fort's guard. The 1927 *Army Manual of Military Training* stated: "Guard duty is considered one of the soldier's most important duties. Upon the proper performance of guard duty depends not only the enforcement of military law and orders, but also the security of persons and property under the charge of the sentinels." (Detroit Historical Museum.)

The Order of the Knights of Columbus is a Catholic fraternal service organization founded in the United States in 1882. It is dedicated to the principles of charity, unity, fraternity, and patriotism. It may be that its patriotic principle led to the establishment of this facility at Fort Wayne. But whether its function was one of recreation for the garrison and open to all, or religious in nature is uncertain. (Detroit Historical Museum.)

This African American bandsman reading the paper outside the old barracks would have served in one of the unit bands assigned to Fort Wayne during World War I. During the war, the fort was headquarters to the 433rd Motor Supply Train and the 430th Troop Transport. A combat unit, the 41st Infantry Regiment was assigned there, as well as construction and labor companies, and a recruit squadron. (Detroit Historical Museum.)

This frame building served as the post's chapel. In 1917, the army determined it needed to train chaplains to staff the forces it was creating for World War I. The resulting U.S. Army Chaplain School was moved several times before being located at Fort Wayne. The school was located in renovated officer housing. Chaplains were trained here from 1922 to 1924 when the school was relocated to Fort Leavenworth, Kansas. (Detroit Historical Museum.)

With the construction of troop barracks outside the star fort in the 1890s, noncommissioned officers and their families moved into the old barracks. This photograph of sergeants and their wives was taken in 1928 at the old barracks. The 1861 renovation that added the brick kitchen and washrooms included the wooden railed verandas in the spaces between the additions providing space for the families to enjoy their leisure hours. (Detroit Historical Museum.)

The 37th Regimental Band from the fort regularly participated in parades in Detroit such as this one in 1921. The 37th Infantry Regiment, organized in 1865 at Fort Wayne as the 19th U.S. Infantry, had arrived from Texas in 1920. In 1921, the 37th absorbed the 54th Infantry Regiment that had marched the 400 miles to Detroit from Camp Grant in Illinois in 20 days. (Detroit Historical Museum.)

In the 1920s, Fort Wayne was a sleepy army garrison post. As this boy lounged beneath a silent cannon on the parade field, officers spent their leisure hours on the fort's nine-hole golf course. Located near the fort's main gate, the course produced a moment of fame for one officer when a strong wind from the Detroit River rolled his slicing shot nearly to Fort Street a half-mile distance. (Detroit Historical Museum.)

At the conclusion of World War I the army looked upon tractor-drawn field artillery pieces as a success in combat and retained motorized artillery as appropriate for wars in countries having extensive road networks. For flexibility however, some 75 millimeter gun units were to remain mule-drawn. This 1928 photograph shows mule-drawn field artillery being inspected on the Fort Wayne parade field. (Detroit Historical Museum.)

North of Detroit, Selfridge Air Base trained pilots during World War I. In the coming years the fighter ace, Eddie Rickenbacker, and Charles Lindbergh, the first man to fly solo across the Atlantic, served at the base. This photograph of the star fort may have been taken by an aircraft from Selfridge. The 607th Aero Squadron was stationed at Fort Wayne until 1919, but whether aircraft accompanied the unit is unknown. (Detroit Historical Museum.)

As the community grew around the fort, military training space became limited. In 1880, the rifle range located a few thousand yards west of the star fort was closed when an errant shot mistakenly hit a ferry boat operating on the Detroit River. In 1926, an army wife wrote that the sally port shown on the right in this photograph had been converted to a machine gun range. (Detroit Historical Museum.)

In 1926, some were proposing the parade field was ideal for an airport. Under favorable wind conditions ordinary aircraft of the period could land at the site. It was suggested that by razing a few buildings, it would be large enough for any aircraft to land under any conditions. The strut of a period aircraft can be seen in this 1930 aerial photograph of the fort. (Detroit Historical Museum.)

By 1928, housing had been built for the families of senior noncommissioned officers serving at the fort. Sitting on the steps is the family of 1st Sergeant Hansen. Next door in the duplex lived Sergeant Rhodes with his family. Both soldiers were assigned to the 2nd Infantry Regiment that garrisoned the fort until August 1940. The second infantry was the last army regiment assigned to Fort Wayne. (Detroit Historical Museum.)

By 1945, firefighting at the fort was the duty of a professionally trained civilian fire department. The post fire department extinguished building fires, provided additional firefighting resources when needed by the local community, and conducted rescue operations, hazardous materials response, as well as emergency medical care. The post fire station was demolished during fort restoration by the historical museum in 1976. (Detroit Historical Museum.)

During World War II, the old star fort was used for vehicle and equipment storage. The slope of the glacis, once an important element of the fort's defenses, remained surrounding the old fort but its purpose had become recreational, as this soldier can be seen practicing his skiing skills, while assigned to the flat landscape of the Detroit region. (Detroit Historical Museum.)

Additional houses which served the fort's senior-level noncommissioned officers were built in 1939. Aligned in a row facing Jefferson Avenue, the homes were collectively referred to as Noncommissioned Officers Row or NCO Row. Each house is a brick two-story duplex providing two bedrooms for each family. The families lived in the homes rent-free with heat, water, and electricity provided by the government. (Detroit Historical Museum.)

In the early years of the fort's existence, social clubs for officers were referred to as open messes, but later became known as officers clubs. This officers club at Fort Wayne situated on the river bank included a sit down dining area, lounges for socializing, meeting rooms, and a bar. Social clubs on army posts are physically separate for commissioned and noncommissioned officers. (Detroit Historical Museum.)

Soldiers were not the first to occupy the area of the fort. Ancient groups of Native Americans often camped here. This burial mound was excavated in 1876 by members of the Detroit Scientific Society and again in 1944 by the Aboriginal Research Club. Pottery and remains indicate the mound dates to the Hopewell culture around 900 AD. These early Americans may have been driven south during the last glacial period. (Detroit Historical Museum.)

The Enlisted Men's Service Club provided an on-post location for the soldiers of the fort to socialize. Like the officers club, this facility provided areas for social activities, dining, meeting rooms, and a bar. The variety of skills the soldiers brought with them from civilian life often provided in-house entertainment as evidenced by this piano player. Separate areas were provided for senior noncommissioned officers and junior enlisted personnel. (Detroit Historical Museum.)

Fort Wayne's post office continued a tradition of military mail dating back to the Egyptian army in 2000 BC. When the fort opened this post office, each military service had its own postal system, which was replaced in 1980 by one Defense Department system. Military mail is subsidized to ensure that correspondence for soldiers does not cost more than normal domestic mail. During some periods, soldiers posted letters without charge. (Detroit Historical Museum.)

All units at the fort kept their small arms in an arms room when not in use. Military weapons, ammunition, and approved privately owned weapons were secured by the unit's armorer. Routine inventory of the weapons, by serial number, were conducted to ensure that all weapons were accounted for by their physical presence or issued to individual soldiers. Small arms repair parts were maintained in the room by the armorer. (Detroit Historical Museum.)

An amendment to the 1944 Surplus Property Disposal Act permitted the military to offer obsolete facilities to governments for preservation. In 1949, the star fort was transferred to the Detroit Historical Museum. Decades later the entire post was placed on the National Register of Historic Places, but throughout the 1950s an active garrison remained beyond the walls of the old fort and decorated Fort Wayne for the holidays. (Detroit Historical Museum.)

In the 1950s, the army developed a recreational program for maintaining soldier morale. The program included drawing and painting; ceramics and sculpture; metal work; leather crafts; model building; photography; and woodworking. These activities took place in well-equipped on-post facilities, such as this woodworking shop at Fort Wayne, known as the "multiple-type crafts shop." (Detroit Historical Museum.)

The army provided for the off-duty needs and interests of the garrison. Between 1946 and 1955, recreation programs were established and staffed by a combination of active duty military and civilians. Active duty enlisted soldiers and officers held military occupational specialties in Special Services and were assigned at every level of command. Later those military occupational specialties were discontinued and civilians operated the recreation programs with military oversight. (Detroit Historical Museum.)

Unit supply rooms on the post maintained stocks of supplies for issue and ordered replacement stocks as needed. Unit supply personnel conducted inventories to account for government property and placed orders to replace lost, damaged, or destroyed items. When units went into the field, the supply clerks coordinated the issue and turn-in of military equipment and transported required supplies to the point of use or issue locations. (Detroit Historical Museum.)

The fort's dispensary was intended to provide outpatient care. Treatment for emergency cases was available, but activities related to the health of the garrison such as physical examinations, immunizations, medical administration, preventive medicine, and sanitary measures were its primary function. Patients whose expected duration of illness exceeded 72 hours were normally kept at the dispensary for only as long as it took to arrange transportation to an area hospital. (Detroit Historical Museum.)

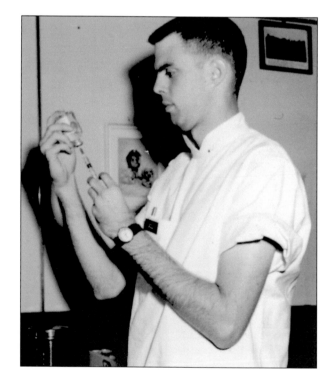

The large rooms in the troop barracks used for serving and eating meals were referred to as mess halls. The term mess referred to a group of military personnel that regularly ate together. This meal being served during the Cold War is far removed from the soldier's rations of beer, beans, prunes, and black coffee issued to troops in 1879 that were expected to supplement them on their $12.75 monthly pay. (Detroit Historical Museum.)

The National Defense Authorization Act requires that the military provide the rendering of military funeral honors for an eligible veteran if requested by the family. The Fort Wayne garrison provided funeral honors for area army veterans. After folding the U.S. flag that draped the coffin as a pall, the officer in charge presented it to the next of kin "on behalf of a grateful nation." (Detroit Historical Museum.)

Prior to 1895, recreational activities for soldiers were provided by civilian groups with expenses met by enlisted men's contributions. No government assistance was involved except permission to occupy vacant buildings. The groups provided food and drink, pool tables, and bowling alleys. Seeking to eliminate the problems associated with liquor at these facilities Congress began appropriating funds for service clubs. The service club at Fort Wayne included a basement bowling alley. (Detroit Historical Museum.)

To improve soldier morale, the army began using military art to decorate day rooms, recreation areas, mess halls, and so on. Many soldier artists volunteered to paint murals. These artists at work were watched by other soldiers who wanted to learn how to paint. In cooperation with civilian art instructors and the local Detroit community, the army responded by providing post facilities to volunteer art instructors. (Detroit Historical Museum.)

Soldiers from Fort Wayne were often called upon to perform ceremonial duties in the metropolitan Detroit area. The color guard here is presenting the colors at the opening night baseball game at Tiger Stadium in April 1963. With the closing of the fort, the duties at these ceremonies are performed by national guard and army reserve units or soldiers of area army recruiting stations. (Detroit Historical Museum.)

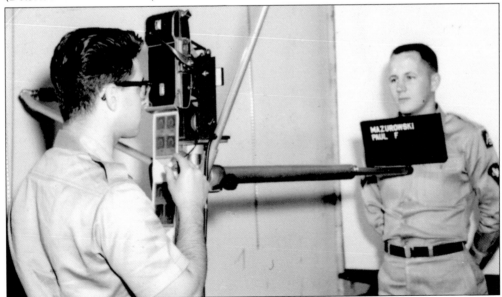

An administrative activity at the fort was issuing a United States Uniformed Services Privilege and Identification Card (United States Military ID); colored green for active duty personnel and red for reservists. The card identifying a person as a member of the armed forces is used to control access to military bases, commissaries, recreation facilities, and high-security areas. Smart cards now allow for automatic building access, communications encryption, and computer access. (Detroit Historical Museum.)

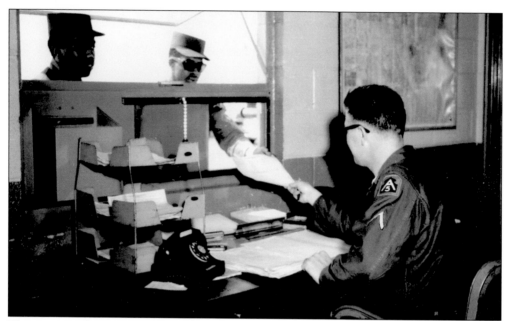

The motor pool was responsible for the army's motorized vehicles. Motor pool operations at the fort included such activities as vehicle repairs, parts cleaning, oil changes, and dispatch. Records were kept on the hours of operation for each vehicle in order to ensure that maintenance was performed to the required schedules. A rigid dispatch system ensured those records were accurate. (Detroit Historical Museum.)

Soldiers volunteering for military service often list education as a major reason for enlisting. To serve that interest and improve the knowledge, aptitude, and confidence of its soldiers, the army developed education centers at each post. Fort Wayne's learning facility provided soldiers with the opportunity to pursue their education through individual study, laboratory work, and tutorial assistance. It also provided individual and unit training to sharpen a soldier's skills. (Detroit Historical Museum.)

Six

DETROIT'S SOCIAL CENTER

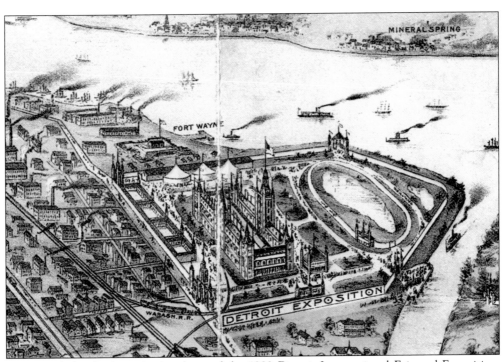

This aerial sketch, from the brochure of the 1889 Detroit International Fair and Exposition, shows the 14-acre site adjoining Fort Wayne and the nearby burgeoning industrial area. Those attending watched sailboat races, baseball games, and viewed art treasures and exhibits of steam powered tractors. Fairgoers were also entertained at the bandstand by Fort Wayne's 7th Infantry Regimental Band. (Detroit Historical Museum.)

The fort's regimental bands, like this group playing on the parade field, were popular entertainment for the garrison and Detroit citizens. In the early 1900s, the leadership of the army requested funds from Congress for the establishment of military bands. The commanders argued that music would improve the "fighting spirit" of the troops. In 1916, Congress passed a bill authorizing bands for artillery, cavalry, and infantry regiments. (Detroit Historical Museum.)

The fort often took on a festive atmosphere in the early days of the Civil War as patriotic citizens took picnic excursions from Detroit to view martial exercises. In the 1890s, Sunday band concerts, formal reviews, and dress parades on the riverfront turned the fort into a social center. The social etiquette of the old army provided officers and their wives with endless courtesy calls, teas, and receptions. (Detroit Historical Museum.)

By the end of the 19th century, Detroit became known as "the mother-in-law" of the army as each departing regiment took with it at least one Detroit society lady as a new bride. Here an officer's wife enjoys a day away from the fort visiting Belle Isle Park on the Detroit River. (Detroit Historical Museum.)

Soldiers leaving the fort for points around Detroit, or visitors arriving, relied on street cars in the fort's early years. Beginning in 1863, horse-drawn street cars made stops at the fort's main gate. From there a system of connecting lines moved throughout the city. Detroit operated the first municipally-owned transit system in the country and street cars, under various modes of power, remained on the Detroit streets until 1956. Inventors were constantly looking for sources to power street cars. The experimental car standing outside the Ford Wayne gate was inventor A. A. Wilder's attempt to replace horse-drawn cars with steam. On its trial run, the car proceeded at the pace of a pedestrian until it reached an ascent. The passengers had to leave the car and push it up the slope. This was not an improvement over horsepower. (Detroit Historical Museum.)

The Fort Wayne Theater, constructed by the Works Progress Administration (WPA) in 1938 showed the popular movies of the day. It had facilities for supporting plays and the stage was even equipped with a wind machine. For soldiers and civilians working demanding hours during World War II, the close proximity and convenient show times provided the opportunity for recreation on the fort's grounds. (Detroit Historical Museum.)

The service club served as a social center for the enlisted soldiers. The facility, built in 1903, has a gymnasium, dining area, and a bowling alley. The club's gym served as space for social functions and physical competition. After the army left Fort Wayne, the facility became the visitor's center for the historic fort. Today it is also used for community events including the biannual Fort Wayne Flea Market. (Detroit Historical Museum.)

The officer's club at Fort Wayne was traditionally the location of social events for the commissioned officers and the citizens of Detroit. In the 1890s, the guests from the city attended dinners hosted by officers attired in stiff formal dress uniforms, high standing collars, spurs, and swords. By the 1940s, the uniforms had become decidedly less formal at these occasions. (Detroit Historical Museum.)

Civilians greatly outnumbered soldiers at the fort during the war years of the 1940s. Here at a picnic held at a nearby park only a few military personnel can be seen enjoying the food and company. Even the privately owned cars are numerous compared to only three military vehicles parked nearby. (Detroit Historical Museum.)

During World War II, a number of the troops stationed at Fort Wayne were natives of Detroit and the surrounding communities. During off duty hours, it was common for their spouses, family members, and particular friends to pay a visit to them at the fort. This photograph of a soldier and his guest was taken on the west glacis of the star fort in the early 1940s. (Detroit Historical Museum.)

Armed Forces Day was celebrated at Fort Wayne, replacing Army Day. This change in 1949 was the result of the unification of the Armed Forces under the Department of Defense. In 1962, in his Armed Forces Day address, Pres. John F. Kennedy provided this, "Word to the Nation: Guard zealously your right to serve in the Armed Forces, for without them, there will be no other rights to guard." (Detroit Historical Museum.)

Seven

ARSENAL OF DEMOCRACY

A battle scene in France, captured by a Fort Wayne soldier, shows the new challenge for the United States and its allies in World War II. As war raged across the globe, Fort Wayne was designated a principal motor supply depot for U.S. forces in 1940. The numbers of parts requisitioned by the fort's military and civilian staff were the result of mathematical calculations made by experts from the United States, Russia, China, Britain, and other allied nations. Mortality ratings were established for nearly 3,000 truck parts based on variations in terrain and climate. The mortality ratings were used to determine the quantities of each component ordered, stockpiled, and distributed to overseas depots and stations. (Detroit Historical Museum.)

During both World War I and World War II, major league baseball players were drafted or enlisted in the armed forces. Detroit Tiger star and the American League's most valuable player in 1940, Hank Greenberg was drafted into military service in 1941. Other baseball stars of the period traveled on USO tours to visit the troops overseas. Fort Wayne's units fielded baseball teams for recreation. (Detroit Historical Museum.)

During World War I, the fort served as a center for transportation and construction units. It was headquarters for the 430th Troop Transport and housed a motorcycle company and an aero squadron. No evidence has been found that the aero squadron quartered at the fort was equipped with aircraft. During World War II, the fort served as a shipping point for thousands of tons of transportation-related war material. Pres. Franklin D. Roosevelt named Detroit the "arsenal of democracy" as the region's automobile companies converted to wartime production. The facilities at Fort Wayne were not sufficient to house the volume of space required to administer the nation's wartime production. Downtown Detroit skyscrapers such as the Guardian and Buhl buildings housed activities coordinating the production of military goods. The 25-story Buhl Building, designed by Wirt Rowland, was constructed in 1925. (Detroit Historical Museum.)

The hospital at Fort Wayne had only limited capacity for the garrison. During times of war returning veterans were treated in area hospitals. One of these facilities was the Henry Ford Hospital, financed and built by Henry Ford in 1915. During World War I, while undergoing an expansion, it was turned over to the federal government for use as U.S. Army General Hospital No. 36, providing care for military personnel. (Detroit Historical Museum.)

The number of civilians employed at Fort Wayne increased from one in October 1940 to 850 a year later. Though the civilians staffing desks that filled orders had no idea where the equipment was actually headed, they were encouraged to provide suggestions aimed at finding better ways to do their jobs. Ideas from the fort's employees ranged from more efficient packing of material to speeding up the order filling process. (Detroit Historical Museum.)

As an ordnance depot, the fort purchased motor vehicles from Michigan plants manufacturing military equipment and distributed them to quartermaster locations overseas. The fort not only handled material, but also all of the fiscal activities associated with motor supplies, equipment, gasoline, and oil for the army's Fifth and Sixth Service Commands. (Detroit Historical Museum.)

At the time the 2nd Infantry Regiment departed Fort Wayne, its band was reputed to be the finest in the U.S. Army. Subsequent army musicians played for military functions and performed at social events at the post. In 1942, a post orchestra provided the music for recreational activities and Works Projects Administration (WPA) dances attended by soldiers at the fort and guests from Detroit. (Detroit Historical Museum.)

Upon the departure of the 2nd Infantry Regiment in August 1940, jurisdiction for the post came under the army's quartermaster department. In September of that year, the 1906 company barracks were used to house two companies of the quartermaster corps and medical and signal corps detachments. In 1942, the fort was transferred to the Ordnance Department but its motor transport responsibilities remained the same. (Detroit Historical Museum.)

The War Department order issued on September 9, 1940, established Fort Wayne as a Motor Supply Depot under command of the quartermaster general. Under its new commander, Lt. Col. E. H. Besse, the fort was expanded with former troop barracks being converted into office buildings. (Detroit Historical Museum.)

When posted for guard duty, members of the fort's guard were instructed: "Take charge of the post and all government property in view; Report all violations of orders I am instructed to enforce; Be especially watchful at night, and during the time for challenging, to challenge all persons on or near my post, and allow no one to pass without proper authority; Quit my post only when properly relieved." (Detroit Historical Museum.)

Soldiers serving at Fort Wayne during World War II were assigned this mess duty commonly referred to as KP for kitchen police. The duty entailed cleaning cooking and eating utensils, floors, and tables; serving food in chow lines; and preparation, though not the cooking of food. While sometimes given as punishment for minor infractions of military rules it was also a necessary duty assigned to enlisted personnel on a rotating basis. (Detroit Historical Museum.)

The Selective Service Act, passed in September 1940, required that no soldiers be sworn into service until the army made adequate provision for housing them. The basic features of central heating, interior showers, and latrines lacking in these tents near the two company barracks would indicate they were not used to house soldiers of the fort, but had been erected as part of military training or as temporary storage. (Detroit Historical Museum.)

Fort Wayne · *Procurement*

TRUCK TRACKS

BY AND FOR THE SOLDIERS AND CIVILIANS OF FORT WAYNE · DETROIT

VOL. II · NO. 19   WEDNESDAY, FEBRUARY 10, 1943   DETROIT, MICHIGAN

Plan Center For Salvage, Reclamation

Col. MacDonald Inspects Sites

As Fort Wayne expands and progresses, so most its various departments of service follow suit.

This is the case of the Fort Wayne Salvage and Reclamation Department and the fact that it has progressed so rapidly since August of 1942 when it had only a two-man department, might be one of the reasons for its latest development.

Lt. Col. W. A. MacDonald, 6th Service Command Salvage and Reclamation Officer, spent a few days on the Post to inspect several possible sites for this new project.

BUY BONDS—BONDS BUY BOMBERS

Fort Takes Raid Alert 'In Stride'

Efficiency Marks 15-Minute Test

Fort Wayne participated in Detroit's fifteen minute air raid alert on Wednesday, February 3. At exactly 10 a.m., the raid siren was blown and all activity other than of a military nature ceased immediately.

Every soldier had his job to do. Whether they were a member of machine gun, rifle or fire fighting crews, everyone calmly but quickly jumped to his post with the serious thought: "This could be the real thing."

Q.M. DETACHMENT ACTIVE

As usual, the boys from the

Early in the war, soldiers at Fort Wayne began publishing an informal post newspaper named *Truck Tracks*. The first editions of the paper devoted more space to the social aspects of army life than war news. The paper carried post rumors, social notes on soldiers and civilian employees, cartoons and jokes, events at the fort, and short biographies of post personnel. Later editions carried more militarily significant articles. (Detroit Historical Museum.)

These women, taking the oath of enlistment as they entered the army at Fort Wayne during World War II, received the same pay as their male counterparts. For enlisted soldiers it was $50 to $138 per month and for officers between $150 and $333. They received free mailing privileges and a 20 percent pay premium for service overseas. Up to 150,000 women served in the Woman's Army Corps during the war. (Detroit Free Press.)

In language of the period, this recruiting pamphlet encouraged recruits, "and every day, every hour, theirs is the deep satisfaction of helping win this war in a woman's way." Women between the ages of 20 and 49, married or single, but without children under the age of 14 largely served in communications, clerical, and service platoons, working as post office clerks, telephone operators, stenographers and typists, motor vehicle drivers, and mechanics. (Detroit Historical Museum.)

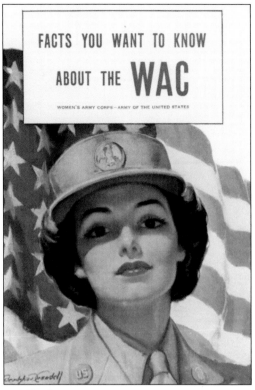

The fort's seven massive warehouses were unable to store the volume of parts managed by the Motor Supply Depot requiring storage at off-site locations such as this one at the Port of Detroit docks. Tires were considered the most precious items. The facilities also stocked parts for 230 motor vehicles, 80,000 different parts for 32 makes of trucks, 11 motorcycle models, 40 trailer models, and 1,300 items of tooling. (Detroit Historical Museum.)

The fort's expanded parade field was the site of a new $800,000 warehouse for the stockpiling and distribution of motor vehicles from Michigan manufacturing companies that retooled commercial product lines for wartime production. The "temporary" facilities were constructed of brick, concrete, and steel. The warehouses on the parade field would remain in place long after the war ended until they were removed by the Detroit Historical Museum in 1976. (Detroit Historical Museum.)

The fort was used as a temporary internment center for Italian prisoners of war captured during the North African Campaign. When the Italian government surrendered to the allies in 1943 and declared war on Germany the following year, the prisoners were designated the Italian Quartermaster Service Unit. The unit worked at Fort Wayne until it was repatriated to Italy in 1945. Later, some former prisoners returned to make their homes in Detroit. (Wayne State University.)

Eight

COLD WAR YEARS

The post headquarters, a two-story brick structure, was constructed in 1905. At the time, the fort was garrisoned by the 1st Infantry Regiment commanded by Capt. Charles E. Tayman and later by Capt. M. T. Swaine. The post commander and the members of his various staff branches were located in this building. The staff was responsible for advising the commander and planning and executing the commander's orders regarding fort operations. (Detroit Historical Museum.)

"COME UNTO ME, YE OPPREST!"
—Alley in the Memphis *Commercial Appeal.*

Following the Bolshevik Revolution and a series of anarchist bombings in 1919, the Red Scare took hold in the United States. The propaganda of communists, socialists, and anarchists caused fears of a Bolshevik-style revolution. Thousands were jailed. Fort Wayne served as a detention center. Lacking a garrison, the prisoners were guarded by veteran's organizations and police. By 1920, the scare had passed and the 37th Infantry Regiment regarrisoned the fort. (Detroit Historical Museum.)

When the second infantry, the last regiment assigned to Fort Wayne, departed in 1940, the troops welcomed the move. Industry near the fort caused pollutants to routinely cover the post making it difficult to keep things clean. Manufacturing changed the atmosphere from the days when Alexander Forman, 7th Michigan, wrote of the fort's idyllic setting: "We have a large Grove for our Parade Ground and general place of recreation." (Detroit Historical Museum.)

At the end of World War II, plans were made to close the fort. In 1948, the star fort was transferred to the City of Detroit for use as a military museum. The temporary frame buildings on the parade ground served as an office, exhibit shops, and artifact storage. On the remainder of the fort, the army positioned a 90-millimeter anti-aircraft artillery battery and located a recruiting center. In 1957, the 28th Artillery Group under the Army Air Defense Command (ARADCOM) upgraded the 90-millimeter anti-aircraft guns it had deployed in the region and replaced them with Nike-Ajax anti-aircraft missiles. Fort Wayne was then tasked with providing maintenance and logistical support for the anti-aircraft missile batteries situated locally to protect the skies of the metropolitan Detroit region. (Detroit Historical Museum.)

The anti-aircraft defenses surrounding Detroit were modernized further when, in 1959, the Army Air Defense Command provided the 28th Artillery Group (Air Defense) with Nike-Hercules missiles to replace the Nike-Ajax system. The Nike-Hercules was a more powerful missile that could carry a nuclear warhead. Fort Wayne now had responsibility for supporting a Detroit air defense that had a nuclear capability. (Detroit Historical Museum.)

During the Korean and Vietnam conflicts, Fort Wayne served as a military induction center. Today called Military Entrance Processing Stations, or MEPS, the stations were then known as Armed Forces Examining and Entrance Stations (AFEES) and were part of the Army Recruiting Command. The two barracks at the fort that served as the induction center were located where the visitors' parking lot is today and were demolished in 1976. (Detroit Historical Museum.)

The Vietnam era saw the need for more people in uniform. To meet personnel needs during Vietnam, the draft was reinstated and the processing of new soldiers from Michigan was done by the United States Army Recruiting Command's Fort Wayne detachment. Today's military is a volunteer force, but as in Vietnam service, members are screened in three areas: aptitude for military service, physical qualification, and background evaluation. (Detroit Historical Museum.)

New recruits were issued military clothing and equipment for which they became financially responsible, including identification (dog) tags, field jackets, shirts, trousers, neckties, canteens, helmets, and shoes. Items were quickly stuffed in barrack bags with a warning to check them later for proper fit. Recruits were reminded to ensure they were issued each required item as claims for missing items would not be allowed once they had departed the building. (Detroit Historical Museum.)

The oath of enlistment into the armed forces is administered by any commissioned officer to persons enlisting in the military. The oath recited by enlisted members is different than the oath of allegiance officers take during commissioning. The officer asks the person to raise their right hand and repeat the oath. The oath is traditionally performed in front of the United States flag as shown in this Fort Wayne ceremony. (Detroit Historical Museum.)

"Shipping out" is part of Fort Wayne's history. During the 1960s, soldiers, including co-author James Conway, destined for South Vietnam, departed the fort. Earlier generations had left to fight expansion wars in the west, rebellion in the south, imperialists in the Philippines, two world wars, and communism on the Korean Peninsula. Most departed hearing a nation's call, others obeying its draft, but all served and many did not return. (Detroit Historical Museum.)

Army units regularly fielded softball and baseball teams with competition becoming, at times, fierce to produce winning teams. Gen. Dwight D. Eisenhower, as a young officer, was frustrated to learn that his ability to coach winning post football teams was consigning him to remain at an assignment he deemed not conducive to career advancement. At Fort Wayne a baseball diamond was laid out on the parade field. (Detroit Historical Museum.)

Early in its history, Fort Wayne controlled other forts throughout the state of Michigan including those at Fort Wilkins, Fort Gratiot, Fort Brady, and Fort Mackinac, but on July 16, 1964, it became a sub-post of Fort Sheridan outside Chicago, Illinois. The garrison turned out for a post ceremony during which Col. Benjamin Chapla took command of the fort and inspected the troops. (Detroit Historical Museum.)

On October 20, 1964, the garrison stood in formation in front of the post headquarters building to listen to the announcement of the death of former president Herbert Hoover. An ex-president for 31 years, Hoover served before most of those listening had been born. Displaying an understanding of the nature of soldiering Hoover had once observed, "Older men declare war. But it is the youth that must fight and die." (Detroit Historical Museum.)

Lt. Gen. Charles G. Dodge, the Fifth Army commander, reviews the troops during a visit to Fort Wayne. In its final years as an active post the fort was organized under the Fifth Army. The fort's missions mirrored those of its parent organization; preparing to mobilize and deploy reserve component units, planning for the security and protection of critical assets, and, when ordered, providing assistance to civilian authorities during emergencies. (Detroit Historical Museum.)

Retreat was a daily ceremony at Fort Wayne during which the nation's flag was lowered at the end of the workday. Everyone within sight or sound of the ceremony came to attention and faced the flag and saluted. Cars stopped and drivers left their vehicles to honor the colors. The retreat ceremony in the American army dates back to the Revolutionary War. Cannon fire and bugle calls accompanied the ceremony. (Detroit Historical Museum.)

Nine

PLACE OF REFUGE

The Great Depression was an economic downturn that started in 1929 and lasted throughout much of the 1930s. The industrialized nations of Europe and the United States felt the greatest impact, but the economic effects were felt worldwide. City dwellers were particularly hard hit with unemployment and homelessness. The old troop barracks at Fort Wayne were used as living space for homeless families. (Detroit Historical Museum.)

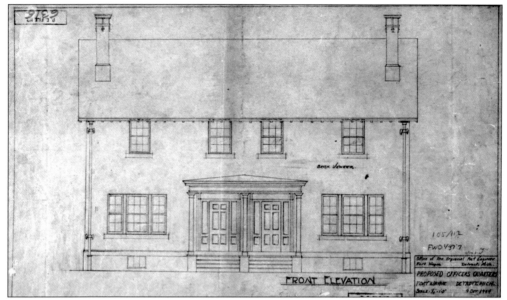

The Works Progress Administration was created in May 1935 to counteract the widespread unemployment that was encountered during the Great Depression. It employed millions of people nationally working on public buildings and roads. When it was closed down by Congress in 1943, it was the largest employer in the United States. Construction projects on the parade field, officers housing, and the old scarp wall were completed by WPA staff. (Detroit Historical Museum.)

In 1937 the Works Project Administration did repair work at the fort, reclaiming land from the river, replacing cracked and deteriorating brick, reconditioning buildings, rebuilding the concrete coping on the scarp wall, and laying 15 acres of new sod. The wooden homes on officer's row were modernized with updated plumbing and electricity. The houses received the brick facing now seen on all but the restored commanding officers home. (Detroit Historical Museum.)

The Works Progress Administration not only renovated existing post facilities, but built new ones as well. The program constructed a new sentry house, post theater, gymnasium, and gasoline station. The total cost of the rehabilitation for the star fort, post buildings, construction, and other activities at the fort totaled $3,213,000. The army paid $932,000 of the costs and the Works Projects Administration covered the remainder. (Detroit Historical Museum.)

The Public Works of Art Project was organized "to give work to artists by arranging to have competent representatives of the profession embellish public buildings." This program was followed in 1935 by the Federal Art Project established by the Works Progress Administration. Before the Federal Art Project ended in 1943, it sponsored a series of martial themed murals at Fort Wayne, completed by Frank Cassara, an Italian born painter and print maker who studied at the Detroit School of Art. After studying fresco painting, Cassara was appointed supervisor of the Michigan easel painting section of the Works Progress Administration's Federal Art Program. His art is displayed in museums in Michigan, Paris, Amsterdam, and at the Smithsonian American Art Museum. His murals at Fort Wayne have probably not survived. (Detroit Historical Museum.)

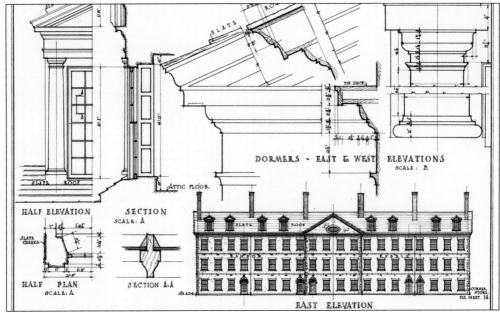

The Historic American Buildings Survey (HABS) was another of the government-sponsored work programs during the Great Depression. Trained architects and engineers were recruited to document achievements in architecture, engineering, and design in the United States. A wide range of building types were selected for documentation in 1933. Among the 35,000 historic structures and sites dating from pre-Columbian times to the 20th century selected was historic Fort Wayne. (Historic American Buildings Survey.)

The Civilian Conservation Corps was a work relief program for young men during the Great Depression. The army was the only government agency with the capability to organize and transport large numbers of men from their homes to program work sites and became involved in the program from its inception. Fort Wayne served as one of the mobilization centers for youth bound for the Civilian Conservation Corps working camps. (NARA.)

During the Great Depression, Fort Wayne had been home to those unable to find shelter for their families. In the 1940s, the fort again became a place of refuge for homeless citizens of the Detroit area. Unused buildings at the fort were opened to the families, but as pointed out in newspaper articles in the *Detroit Free Press*, the buildings needed to be renovated before they could become suitable dwellings. (Detroit Free Press.)

The newly reopened building at the fort had particular dangers for children. Unsanitary facilities and exposed wiring were identified as areas requiring action to protect those living there. The fort would become a home for citizens in 1967 when civil unrest in Detroit resulted in the displacement of families. Families whose homes had been destroyed in the violence would remain at the fort for years, the last leaving in 1971. (Detroit Free Press.)

The enlisted service club served for a time as a job services facility. The program was designed to involve low-income students in a career development process and to assist them in acquiring the skills needed to achieve their goals. Integrated in the process were academic, vocational, and social skills training. The program is no longer located at the fort. (Detroit Historical Museum.)

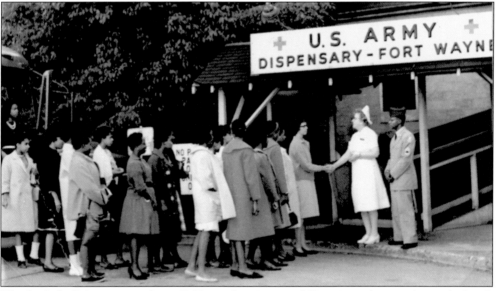

The fort's facilities were made available to the citizens of Detroit as the army's use declined. The dispensary provided outreach medical programs. The officer's club, for a period, housed the Mosaic Youth Theatre, a nonprofit organization providing free professional training in singing, acting, and technical theater to Detroit-area youths. The theater left the fort in 2004 when the lack of a workshop limited opportunity for technical theater education. (Detroit Historical Museum.)

Ten

HISTORIC FORT WAYNE

The U.S. Army Corps of Engineers still operates a 13-acre boatyard in the fort's southeast corner. There the yard's civilian employees help maintain shipping channels along the eastern shore of Michigan. This view shows tugs, survey boats, and dredges laid up for the winter in the yard's riverside slip. (Detroit Historical Museum.)

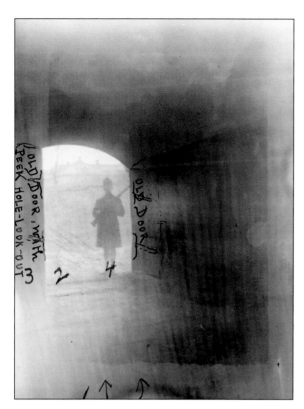

This unique image, from the private collection of a family long connected with Fort Wayne, is said to capture the ghostly apparition of a Civil War–era sentry at the fort's main sally port entrance. The presence of Barracks 311 in the background places the date of the photograph at sometime after 1894. (Private collection in memory of Fort Wayne's veterans.)

The stone arched entrance, dating from the Civil War–era renovations, was the old fort's visitors' main entrance from the museum's opening in 1949. This view shows the imposing 22-foot high scarp wall facing the original dry moat or ditch which completely surrounds the old star fort. (Detroit Historical Museum.)

From 1949 until 2006, the Fort Wayne Military Museum was operated by the Detroit Historical Museum. The cover of this early brochure shows a pre-World War II aerial view of the site. During the early years, admission was free to the public. Since early 2006, the fort has been operated by the Detroit Recreation Department, assisted by the Friends of Fort Wayne organization, the Historic Fort Wayne Coalition, and the Detroit Historical Society. (Detroit Historical Museum.)

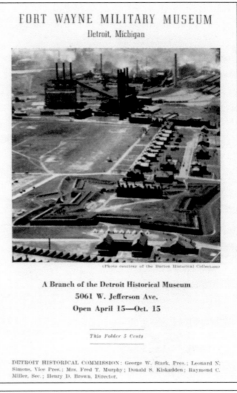

FORT WAYNE MILITARY MUSEUM
Detroit, Michigan

(Photo courtesy of the Burton Historical Collection)

A Branch of the Detroit Historical Museum
5061 W. Jefferson Ave.
Open April 15—Oct. 15

This Folder 5 Cents

DETROIT HISTORICAL COMMISSION: George W. Stark, Pres.; Leonard N. Simons, Vice Pres.; Mrs. Fred T. Murphy; Donald S. Kiskadden; Raymond C. Miller, Sec.; Henry D. Brown, Director.

The weekend known as Pioneer Days was an annual fort summer event from the 1950s to the 1970s. Costumed reenactors and period craft demonstrations were popular attractions. Note the World War II wooden buildings located on the old fort parade ground until they were removed in 1976. (Detroit Historical Museum.)

117

The large ballroom located on the second floor of the 1905 headquarters building was restored to its original appearance and usefulness by the Detroit Historical Museum staff in the late 1970s. Since the museum staff left the building in the 1990s, the grand space has been partitioned off into modern classrooms to serve as the Detroit Head Start teacher training school. (Detroit Historical Museum.)

After the last section of the fort was acquired from the U.S. Department of Interior by the Detroit Historical Museum in 1976, several surplus buildings were demolished. In this view, spectators watch a crane dismantle the Bachelor Officers Quarters. The removal of this building allowed the fort's original protecting earth slope or glacis to be rebuilt. (Detroit Historical Museum.)

The American Bicentennial celebration of 1976 witnessed a grand reopening of restored Fort Wayne—but only for one day in July due to City of Detroit budget constraints. Here the fort's curator, Dr. William Phenix (second from left), accompanies Detroit mayor Coleman A. Young; Mayor Bert Weeks of Windsor, Ontario; an Abraham Lincoln look-alike; and a uniformed Civil War reenactor. (Detroit Historical Museum.)

During excavations for the construction of the Downtown Detroit People Mover elevated railway in the 1980s, several graves of the War of 1812 soldiers were discovered. The Fort Wayne staff organized a formal reburial ceremony, complete with a horse-drawn cortege. The procession left the fort and brought the bodies to their final interment at nearby Woodmere Cemetery on West Fort Street. (Detroit Historical Museum.)

The military section at Woodmere Cemetery, near Fort Wayne in southwest Detroit, contains the many graves removed from the Fort Wayne Cemetery. Rows of military headstones flank the statue of a Civil War soldier. (Photograph by Bob Briggs.)

For several years, the fort hosted the Detroit Public Schools' Junior Reserve Officer Training Corps (JROTC) Field Day. Here uniformed high school students, over a thousand in number, pass in review in front of army officers leading the program and the Detroit Historical Museum's director and other staff. The 1983 event featured army rangers rappelling from helicopters onto the fort's parade field. (Detroit Historical Museum.)

Summer evening riverfront concerts were a popular attraction at the fort in the 1980s. Music ran the gamut from patriotic, jazz, gospel, and bluegrass, to a one-time performance by the Detroit Symphony Orchestra. (Detroit Historical Museum.)

Events on the fort's riverfront parade ground frequently featured the added interest of the passing parade of commercial shipping on the Great Lakes. A part of the St. Lawrence Seaway system, the Detroit River was once the world's busiest commercial waterway. Here cannoneers salute a passing freighter. (Detroit Historical Museum.)

The restoration of the fort's 1880 Commanders Residence was a major museum project in the early 1980s. At the stage seen here, crews have stripped off the 1930s Works Progress Administration (WPA) brick exterior to expose the earlier 1920s red-and-white asbestos shingles. The restoration took six years and cost more than $600,000. (Detroit Historical Museum.)

Since the fort opened as a military museum in 1949, tens of thousands of school children and adults have received guided tours. Here a summertime student guide, costumed as a Civil War–era laundress, takes a group down the sloping original road into the old star fort in the 1980s. (Detroit Historical Museum.)

Because the fort is the location of a thousand-year-old Native American burial mound, it holds a special place in the hearts of Detroit-area Native Americans. This photograph shows a children's dance competition held during one of the powwows held on the riverfront parade ground during the 1980s. (Detroit Historical Museum.)

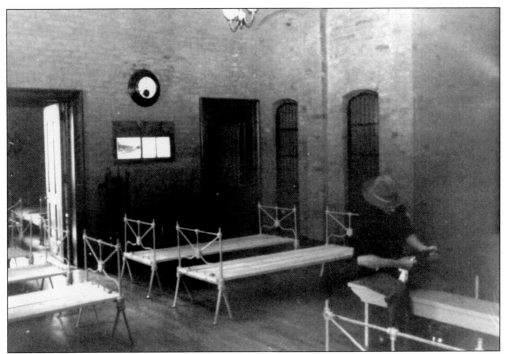

The fort's restored 1889 guardhouse was dedicated and opened in 1983. The interior features authentic high security cells for prisoners and replica iron bunks. Period reenactors continue to spend nights in the building during weekend events. Heat for the building is provided by an original army wood-burning stove. (Detroit Historical Museum.)

As a major Civil War reenactment center in the 1970s and 1980s, the Fort Wayne riverfront parade grounds witnessed many competitions by teams firing muskets and cannons at targets. The friendly rivalry between Union and Confederate units usually drew large crowds of spectators like those seen on the bleachers here. (Detroit Historical Museum.)

The fort curator adopted an African Goose as a pet in the 1980s. The bird raised the alarm with a loud squawking when it sighted visitors. Here it bravely defends the curator's driveway against a crowd of interested visitors. (Detroit Historical Museum.)

During its operation as a military museum in the 1980s, the fort's main entrance was enhanced by the addition of flanking rows of flagpoles and a large overhead sign. The two white flags on the poles nearest the fence are the flag of the United States Army. The poles behind fly the flags of the other American military services: the U.S. Air Force, the U.S. Navy, the Marine Corps, and the Coast Guard. (Detroit Historical Museum.)

Since its opening in 1989, the fort has been home to the National Museum of the Tuskegee Airmen. Using many original artifacts, the museum tells the heroic story of the African American Army aviation unit that served in World War II. Airmen in the segregated unit trained at Alabama's Tuskegee Institute and other bases. Many of the original unit veterans continue to volunteer and give tours at the museum, located adjacent to the fort's gate. (Detroit Historical Museum.)

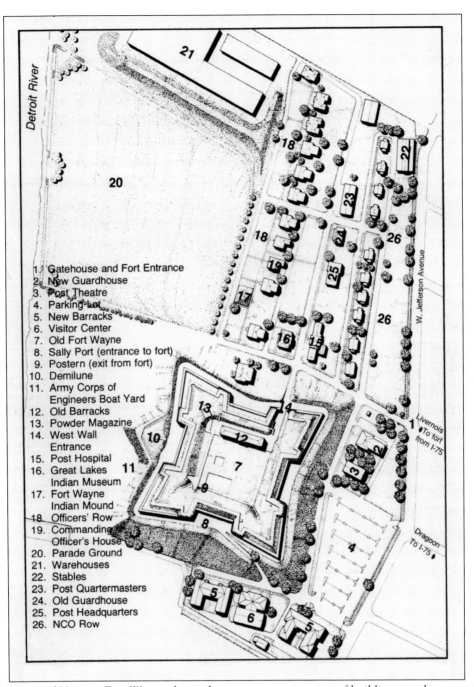

1. Gatehouse and Fort Entrance
2. New Guardhouse
3. Post Theatre
4. Parking Lot
5. New Barracks
6. Visitor Center
7. Old Fort Wayne
8. Sally Port (entrance to fort)
9. Postern (exit from fort)
10. Demilune
11. Army Corps of
    Engineers Boat Yard
12. Old Barracks
13. Powder Magazine
14. West Wall
    Entrance
15. Post Hospital
16. Great Lakes
    Indian Museum
17. Fort Wayne
    Indian Mound
18. Officers' Row
19. Commanding
    Officer's House
20. Parade Ground
21. Warehouses
22. Stables
23. Post Quartermasters
24. Old Guardhouse
25. Post Headquarters
26. NCO Row

This plan of Historic Fort Wayne shows the current arrangement of buildings on the grounds. The list at left identifies the site's key buildings. Note that the Detroit River's shore forms the southern edge of the 83-acre property. The international border with Canada is located in the middle of the river. An unusual fact is from Detroit, the United States actually lies to the north of Ontario, Canada. The "fort at Springwells, near Detroit" was established to protect the citizens of Detroit. That mission accomplished, Fort Wayne today preserves the military and Native American heritage of its people.

DISCOVER THOUSANDS OF LOCAL HISTORY BOOKS FEATURING MILLIONS OF VINTAGE IMAGES

Arcadia Publishing, the leading local history publisher in the United States, is committed to making history accessible and meaningful through publishing books that celebrate and preserve the heritage of America's people and places.

Find more books like this at
www.arcadiapublishing.com

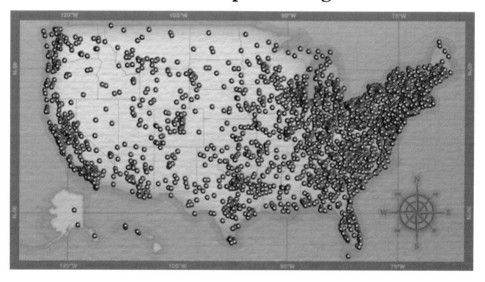

Search for your hometown history, your old stomping grounds, and even your favorite sports team.

Consistent with our mission to preserve history on a local level, this book was printed in South Carolina on American-made paper and manufactured entirely in the United States. Products carrying the accredited Forest Stewardship Council (FSC) label are printed on 100 percent FSC-certified paper.

MADE IN THE USA